Ritual Practice in Modern Japan

Ritual Practice in Modern Japan

Ordering Place, People, and Action

Satsuki Kawano

 University of Hawai'i Press

Honolulu

10 09 08 07 06 05   6 5 4 3 2 1

Library of Congress Cataloging-in-Publication Data

Kawano, Satsuki.
     Ritual practice in modern Japan : ordering place, people,
and action / Satsuki Kawano.
            p. cm.
     Includes bibliographical references and index.
     ISBN 0-8248-2877-1 (hardcover : alk. paper) —
ISBN 0-8248-2934-4 (pbk. : alk. paper)
1. Rites and ceremonies—Japan—Kamakura-shi. 2. Festivals—
Japan—Kamakura-shi. 3. Fasts and feasts—Japan—Kamakura-shi.
4. Kamakura-shi (Japan)—Religious life and customs. 5. Kamakura-shi
(Japan)—Social life and customs. I. Title.
GN635.J2K39 2005
306.4'0952'136—dc22

                                                                    2004026559

Designed by University of Hawai'i Press production staff
Printed by The Maple-Vail Book Manufacturing Group

Contents

Acknowledgments

Although many people helped me to complete this work, I am particularly indebted to my mentors for their nurturance. L. Keith Brown has been an everlasting source of encouragement and intellectual challenge at every stage. Andrew Strathern, Richard Scaglion, Thomas Rimer, and Akiko Hashimoto provided valuable guidance and support, and I am deeply grateful.

I would like to acknowledge a number of fellowships and grants that made it possible for me to work on this project. During the initial stage, the Japan Council of the University of Pittsburgh provided a travel grant to conduct a pilot study and to purchase research equipment for fieldwork. The Japan Foundation generously funded my fourteen months of fieldwork in Kamakura between 1995 and 1996. An Andrew Mellon Predoctoral Fellowship (1996–1997) and a Social Science Research Council Dissertation Write-up Fellowship (1996–1997) supported the initial writing stage of this project. A senior fellowship (1998–1999) at the Divinity School at Harvard University provided me with an opportunity to convert my dissertation into an early version of the book manuscript.

While working on this project I received assistance from a number of guides, colleagues, and friends. During fieldwork, Professor Suenari Michio kindly arranged my affiliation at the University of Tokyo. I would like to thank Lawrence Sullivan for providing me with a wonderful interdisciplinary working environment at Harvard University. Misty Bastian has provided me with much encouragement and friendship since we met in Cambridge. The final stages of this work could not have been completed without the generous support and intellectual stimulation of my colleagues and students in the anthropology department at the University of Notre Dame. Among them my special thanks go to Susan Blum and James McKenna for their guidance and encouragement. I would also like to thank John Traphagan for many years of friendship and input.

This book has benefited greatly from Don Yoder's copyediting work. Anonymous reviewers provided constructive comments and suggestions, for which I am also grateful. And my deep gratitude goes to Patricia Crosby at the University of Hawai'i Press for her professionalism and support.

Finally, my heartfelt thanks go to the people who participated in this study. This book would not have been possible without their kindness and generosity.

Introduction

One warm afternoon, Suzuki-*san* and I were sitting in a small café in Kamakura, a medium-sized city near Tokyo. Suzuki-*san* is a thirty-eight-year-old man who works for a pharmaceutical company in Tokyo. He told me: "I do not believe in Shinto or Buddhism. I do not go to shrines or temples for religious reasons. Christian doctrines taught me that I should follow God, but not *kami* [deities, often associated with Shinto] and *hotoke* [buddhas and ancestors]."

Having converted to Christianity when he was in college, Suzuki-*san* maintains no domestic altars enshrining ancestors and tutelary *kami* at home, the central sites for ritual activity in Kamakura. Suzuki-*san* is exceptional, not only because Christianity is a minor religion in Japan (just 1.4 percent of the entire population are Christians),[1] but also because he believes that his ritual actions must be supported by his personal faith. In contrast, most of the people I met in Kamakura tended to downplay personal faith in specific religious doctrines when explaining their ritual actions, such as praying to the tutelary *kami* or ancestors for health and protection. In fact, Japanese people today are known to emphasize "the primacy of action" over belief in explaining their ritual actions (Reader 1991, 15, 20). It is customary for families to belong to Buddhist temples, and many value memorial rites conducted by Buddhist priests to venerate ancestors. Nevertheless, it is not unknown for people to lack knowledge of the Buddhist tradition *(shū)* to which their family temple belongs.[2] In Kamakura, too, ritual actors are more frequently concerned with praying for the well-being of themselves and those close to them, both living and dead, than with theological issues. The attitude of "do it and see if it works" is widespread. And perform-

1

ing rituals might eventually lead to personal commitment to religious ideas and doctrines.

The primacy of action is also evident in recent survey results. They indicate that there are many more ritually active people than those who say they believe in religion or *kami* and *hotoke*. Typically, only one-third or fewer report that they have a religion/religions in which they believe, and approximately two-fifths believe in the existence of *kami* or *hotoke*.[3] Yet many more respondents reported that they visit Buddhist temples or Shinto shrines during New Year holidays and family graves, often located in Buddhist temple compounds, at least once a year.[4] According to the 1998 NHK (Nihon Hōsō Kyōkai, or Japan Broadcasting Corporation) survey, some 81 percent of the respondents reported that they reverently face *(ogamu)* or pray to *kami* and *hotoke* at least once a year (Onodera 1999, 55). The 2001 *Yomiuri Newspaper* survey indicates that some 78 percent of its respondents maintain domestic altars to *kami* or *hotoke* (*Yomiuri Newspaper,* 28 December 2001, 15).[5]

Thus we cannot assume that religious rites are expressions or confirmations of belief in the doctrine regarding supernatural entities and powers. Rather than treating belief and ritual action as self-evident analytical categories and assuming that the former causes the latter, their relationship must be investigated as being culturally constructed and socially generated. In Kamakura, rather than a prerequisite, a personal conviction of or belief in *kami*'s or *hotoke*'s power is just one of the possible consequences of ritual practice. Ritual's persistence and relevance owe much to ritual forms that can create an elevated context infused with a sense of moral order pervasive in daily life. Common ritual actions performed in Kamakura can simultaneously engage ritual actors in special contexts set apart from daily life while evoking moral personhood cultivated in mundane bodies and environments.

When commenting on the small number of believers in religion compared with the number of ritual practitioners, some argue that Japan is a completely secular society, and thus that religion has little relevance to people's lives, while others say ritual practitioners lack awareness that they have a religion because it revolves around conventional rites intertwined with daily life. Neither a meaningless formality nor mere custom, ritual potentially, rather than automatically, provides contemporary urbanites with culturally significant ways of constructing meaning and power. In short, this book aims to demonstrate that people's ritual bodies and environments provide fertile ground for nurturing diverse yet culturally patterned interpretive possibilities and for producing engaging moments of personal significance.

Approaches to Ritual

Rituals are more than repetitive, stylized, prescribed behavior or the social routine. For instance, I do not want to use the analytical category of ritual to examine taking out garbage in Kamakura, even though it fits with a common anthropological definition of ritual in a number of ways: it happens regularly at fixed times and places and involves rigid, prescribed rules and procedures about how to put it together, pile it up, and clean up the collection site. Such descriptions apply to many other aspects of social life or individual habits (see Goody 1977). I certainly do not mean to deny the usefulness of "secular rituals" as an analytical category—formalities that "can present unquestionable doctrines and can dramatize social/moral imperatives without invoking the spirits at all" (Moore and Myerhoff 1977, 3). Graduation ceremonies in Kamakura, for example, fit nicely into this group. Yet, rather than examining secular formalities, this book investigates religious rites, or those often defined by their associations with supernatural entities and powers (such as *kami* and *hotoke* in case of Kamakura) and analyzes the ways in which people construct ritual's multiple interpretive possibilities.[6] Depending on the situation and whom we ask, ritual encounters with *kami* or *hotoke* can be religious occasions of devotion, social occasions of bonding, or formal occasions with little religious value. And some of these characterizations are not necessarily mutually exclusive. Although anthropologists have often studied both the religious and the social implications of religious rites, it has not been uncommon for them to assume that practitioners hold belief in "supernatural" powers and entities associated with religious rites. Then what difference does it make to our understanding of ritual if people state that they do *not* believe in associated powers and entities or religious doctrines? Though people in Kamakura do not always consider *kami* and *hotoke* "supernatural" in the strict sense of the term, they still acknowledge them socially and are aware of their potentially beneficial and destructive aspects. Despite such acknowledgment, we cannot assume that people always find religious importance in rituals involving these beings and powers; and the matter is complex, because even nonbelievers I met told me that sometimes rituals become personally meaningful occasions of emotional engagement in both social and religious terms.

There are several ways of dealing with this issue of belief, though they are not limited to the following list. First, one could avoid the issue of what people say—ritual's meaning—and study only what they do—their ritual activity. This approach is unattractive to me, given my interest in discovering what difference ritual makes to people's lives. Second, one might maintain that people follow conventions and mechanically reproduce ritual actions without recognizing their significance. This account is inconsistent with my observation that people seriously engage in ritual activity and care much about how it is done. Third, one might claim that people do not say they believe in religion but actually do believe in it without knowing they do. By discrediting their accounts of themselves and their actions, this problematic view would portray people as mindless enactors of convention incapable of understanding what they do. Both what people do and what they say matter.

In order to comprehend ritual action in Kamakura, I turn to "practice theories" in anthropology because they illuminate the relationship between people's views of ritual activity and their ritual action.[7] Just as Japanese people tend to emphasize the power of doing, so practice theories highlight the ways in which performance brings categories, ideas, and values into action, thereby (re)producing them. At the same time, practice itself may change these very values and ideas by exposing them to contestation, manipulation, and modification. With practice theories, moreover, ritual actors receive credit for their agency in reproducing as well as changing cultural forms. This perspective stands in sharp contrast to earlier views that regarded actors as powerless pawns following some preassigned scheme. Ritual actors are now seen as active participants who use ritual forms strategically to their advantage. Participants are reported to use rituals to enhance their status (Bloch 1987; Nelson 2000) or to resist authority through collective violence in times of rapid social change (Schnell 1999). Emphasizing the agency of social actors, practice theories criticize the view that rituals thoughtlessly reproduce established ideas, such as religious beliefs, doctrines, and ideologies. Thus, they question certain long-standing concepts in Western thought —for instance, that thought belongs to the mind and that the mind is superior to the body and its actions.

Rituals are often said to create a sense of togetherness in the social world while also maintaining the status quo in a society—with or without the participants' knowledge. But if we are to treat people as active agents capable of strategic participation in rituals, their actions need to make sense to them (cf. Staal 1975). Recent anthropological studies highlight the process in which ritual becomes politically appropriated as a form of performance (Aggarwal 2001; Albro 2001; Mines 2002). Ritual participants, then, need to understand ritual's usefulness in a practical sense in order to use it as an instrument to their advantage.

In examining ritual's meaning and power, I will focus on nonspecialists' accounts, because it is not just specialists and the committed who (re)produce, maintain, and modify rituals. On the contrary, actions of the majority who are nonspecialists determine rituals' survival or decline in a significant way. Their perspectives and knowledge are as critical as specialists' views in understanding ritual's (re)production and power; so we cannot dismiss the accounts of the religiously uncommitted as irrelevant or inferior to the theological accounts offered by ritual leaders and specialists.

Over the course of Japan's history, many schools of Shinto emerged, whereas various traditions of Buddhism came to Japan from the Asian mainland and saw further developments and change. Yet, most people I met knew little about the various schools of Shinto, and nobody mentioned them when explaining their actions at a Shinto shrine or at the domestic altar to *kami*. People sometimes discussed various traditions of Buddhism of their family's affiliation (such as Nichiren-*shū*) and commented on certain components in their ritual styles (such as "we do rituals with lots of drumming"), but they rarely discussed theological issues. A Zen priest in his fifties even told me that the gap between priests' and parishioners' religious worldviews is so great that he feels there is no overlap. Although this is an extreme opinion, despite a number of continuities, both informants and scholars reported certain discontinuities in religious knowledge and concerns between specialists and nonspecialists. Given this difference in perspective, I would like to focus on nonspecialists' views as complements to institutional or specialists' views. This approach also makes sense considering the extent of scholarship on religion and ritual in contemporary Japan that has an institutional emphasis: there are many useful studies of Buddhism and Shinto (to name recent anthropological studies, e.g., Littleton 2002 and

Nelson 2000) and of organizations and followers of the so-called New Religions (e.g., Davis 1980; Earhart 1989; Guthrie 1988; Hardacre 1986; McVeigh 1997).[8]

In seeking to discover ritual's importance among the religiously uncommitted, this book deals with both Shinto and Buddhist practices in which they commonly participate. Shinto, the native religious tradition, and Buddhism, officially brought to Japan in the sixth century, were combined for more than a thousand years. People were Shintoists and Buddhists at the same time, though they did not necessarily see themselves as belonging to two separate religions. The Meiji State (1868–1912) attempted to separate the two officially, yet in today's Japan the separation remains incomplete in practice (R. J. Smith 1974, 15). Despite certain tensions and conflicts, but with no major religious wars between them to eliminate one or the other, Shinto and Buddhist traditions interacted, and theologies reconciling the two traditions came to flourish (ibid., 12). As a result, mutual influence led to a complex orchestration and integration of native and indigenized foreign practices without completely eliminating distinctions between the two traditions. Given the history of blending Shinto and Buddhism and a persistent practice of combining the two traditions in the daily life of many contemporary Japanese, I examine both Shinto and Buddhist rites that are relevant to them.[9] In addition, since various rites in contemporary Japan, such as weddings, festivals, and death and memorial rites, have been examined in detail by others (Ashkenazi 1993; Edwards 1989; Hardacre 1997; Schnell 1999; R. J. Smith 1974; Suzuki 2000), I will emphasize the role that certain ritual forms and frameworks play in uniting these various facets of ritual action, rather than focusing on a specific ritual or a single tradition.

Understanding Ritual Practice in Kamakura

In Kamakura, ritual bodies and environments provide a common source of meaning, uniting different spheres of ritual action and contributing to ritual's multiple, patterned interpretive possibilities. The production of ritual contexts owes much to the use of actions and environments that resonate with—or differentiate them from—the daily routine. Rituals use bodily practices that are common in daily life—bowing, cleaning, giving, receiving—in a higher context (Chapter 2). Bowing to *kami* and ancestors, for example, is interpreted in relation to the bowing done in daily life. Ritual actions, therefore, orient participants toward experiences beyond the immediate ritual context and link them to meanings in everyday life. In other words, acting bodies *embody* ideas and values that everyday practices evoke. Thus the body becomes a site for communicating complex thoughts and values, challenging earlier views that dismiss the body as an animal-like, instinctive part of a person (Farnell 1995, 18, 23). This, in turn, brings us to question the mind/body dichotomy and the superiority of mind over body in considering the value and functions of ritual action.[10]

The creation of ritual contexts comes, not only from acting bodies, but also from the environments that contain them. Bodies do not act in a vacuum. Whether in a house, a neighborhood, or a shrine, it is necessary to take ritual environments as seriously as the ritual bodies that act in them (compare, e.g., with Casey 1996; De Boeck 1998; Feld and Basso 1996; Kahn 1996, 2000; Lovell 1998; Rodman 1992). In both ritual and everyday life, just as bodies are hierarchically ordered, so places are ordered according to upper/lower, front/back, and interior/exterior distinctions that are tied to contrasting cultural meanings such as purity/impurity, formality/informality, and respect/disrespect (Chapter 3). Interacting ritual body and ritual site mutually constitute each other, producing and reproducing cultural dispositions in which body and place are embedded.

Pierre Bourdieu maintains that the habitus, "the durably installed generative principles of regulated improvisations" (1977, 78), is formed in a person as he or she grows up (81) and produces "a commonsense world" (80) for those who share the same habitus. The habitus provides continuity from one situation to another for a person, as well as producing regularities in social life over time (82). Such routine (re)production of actors' subjectivities occurs in the use of the ritual body as well as place. Thus the habitus takes bodily and *emplaced* forms.[11] Because rituals involve bodily actions and environments that are commonly used in everyday life, people may refer to their meaning—such as (dis)-respect, (im)purity, and (in)formality—when interpreting ritual actions and environments. When this occurs, ritual can empower a sense of order that prevails in everyday life by producing a privileged body (Bell 1992) as well as a privileged environment. Because it possibly crystallizes what feels good and thus right in Japanese social life, ritual can produce an occasion of emotional engagement[12] with or without detailed theological knowledge.[13]

Connections among places that constitute the community of Kamakura may also become a source of ritual's meaning. Like a room, a house, or a shrine, Kamakura consists of upper/lower, front/back, and exterior/interior zones that interact with its history as a former capital and resort to generate yet another layer of meaning (Chapter 4). According to the image of Kamakura as an ancient capital, the northern area associated with medieval warriors and their political organization is considered "higher" than the southern communities, which are associated with commoners. According to the image of the city as a prestigious resort, the beach area that formerly housed upper-class summerhouses and resort hotels becomes a "high" place. Participants draw localized meanings and valuations from a constellation of places within Kamakura.

Yet it is not ritual's symbolic potential alone that helps participants to construct the meanings ritual can generate—whether a sense of harmony or a communal identity (Chapter 5). Ritual demands that participants act in specific ways, and a native understanding of practice maintains that performing ritual with sincerity may lead to an understanding and appreciation of what that ritual embodies, however empty it may seem at the beginning. People's interpretations of ritual are diverse, however, and participating in a ritual does not mean that people accept the same unambiguous meanings (Bell 1992, 183). Ritual, then, offers an interesting political potential to various groups, whether those in power or the oppressed, although its implications differ depending on who is using it. By performing ritual, people can create a context in which ritual actors appear to submit to its demands, making ritual a tool for appropriation rather than a mechanism for direct control or indoctrination (see Bell 1992). Through ritualization, people fashion a strategic context for interaction and appropriation for diverse purposes (Chapter 6).

In short, then, the people I met in Kamakura find meaning in the ways in which they use the ritual body, the immediate ritual site, and places beyond it. People's ritual bodies and environments provide a common interpretive framework that brings together their encounters with *kami* and *hotoke* in a range of contexts.

Historical Contexts

Examining a smaller number of believers in religion despite a comparatively larger number of ritual practitioners, some scholars of Japan have characterized the Japanese people as unreligious or areligious, while others have thought that the Japanese are religious in their own way. Whether they characterize the Japanese as religious or not, scholars have often noted how religion in Japan is integrated into social life, as a result of which practitioners might fail to recognize their religion as a category set apart from social conventions (Ishii 1997, 3; Kaneko 1988, 101–102; Ōmura 1988, 15; Shimada 1991, 168; Yanagawa 1991, 10–12). The intertwined nature of religion and social conventions in Japan is described by a variety of phrases: religion without belief (Yanagawa 1991); religion as conventional events (Miyata 1999, 4); religion as action, or something one learns to do (*tashinamu;* Ōmura 1988, 16); "natural" religion without a founder (Ama 1996, 67–68); family religion (Kimura 2003, 145); or religion built on kinship and territorial relations among people (Shimada 1991, 181). While those scholars have highlighted significant aspects of religion and ritual in modern Japan, our understanding of ritual practice in today's Kamakura will benefit further from situating the issue of many ritual practitioners but fewer believers in religion in recent history and relations of power. By stressing certain historical continuities and change before and after World War II, this brief sketch will show that the number of believers reported in surveys declined in postwar Japan in changing political, economic, and social contexts.

In describing these changes, I would like to use Nakada-*san*'s life course as a point of reference. Born in 1923, Nakada-*san* is married to a tea merchant from Kamakura and was seventy-two years old at the time of my fieldwork between 1995 and 1996. As she was growing up, ultra-nationalists established a firmer hold on the Japanese government and widely propagated the national ideology of State Shinto, defining the emperor as living *kami* and Japan as a divine nation. Nakada-*san* was sixteen years old when World War II broke out in 1939. In those days, the state urged the empire's subjects to sacrifice themselves for the nation and the emperor, the divine father figure to whom they were indebted. Ritually, people were encouraged to pray for Japan's prosperity and honor the emperor, his divine ancestors, and the war dead at domestic altars and community shrines. Thus the state imposed patriotic meanings on certain ritual actions.[14] The state permitted religious freedom as long as people and organizations honored the official discourse of ritual, and took disciplinary measures in cases of nonconformity. By the time Nakada-*san* reached her teens, many new religious movements had developed, characterized by charismatic leadership, advocating social reforms, and blending established and folk religious elements. The state exerted a particularly tight control over these religious organizations and required the amendment of their doctrines if they challenged the state-sanctioned framework of ritual. Nonconforming organizations risked imprisonment of their leaders and destruction of their facilities. The Ministry of Education's 1940 survey results illustrate these ideological influences of the time and give us an insight into ritual's meaning in prewar Japan at a time when large-scale national surveys on religion were rare. The survey asked twenty-year-old male respondents to choose the closest feeling to what they experienced when reverently facing *kami* and *hotoke*.[15] Some 48 percent reported that they did so "in order to pray for the prosperity of the Japanese empire." Education at the time aimed to indoctrinate young people into the national ideology, and we find its influence in the survey results.

Nevertheless, the state's policies in prewar Japan by no means exhausted other interpretive possibilities, nor did they homogenize ritual practice among all people. Rather than simply swallowing the state ideology, some people reported that they privately contested state-sanctioned meanings of ritual. According to an eighty-eight-year-old woman, for instance, her deceased father used to say that he was never indebted to the emperor. And Nakada-*san* recalled that "People whose family members were drafted used to go to Shinto shrines to pray for their safe return." Thus, others might have focused more on personally significant reasons for praying at domestic altars and shrines, though such reasons did not have to contradict patriotic meanings of ritual.

A major shift in the official paradigm of ritual action followed Japan's defeat in World War II. When the war ended in 1945, Nakada-*san* was twenty-two years old. Not only did the emperor announce to the public that he was human, but the very idea of his divinity officially became a taboo. Among the public there was also a sense that, despite their prayers, divine powers had failed to protect the nation. In postwar Japan, a new "democratic" paradigm of ritual emerged, and today the state no longer officially defines ritual's meaning. The new constitution ensures people's full-scale freedom of thought and religion. Separation of church and state had occurred.[16] These changes in postwar Japan provide a point of reference for people today in constructing ritual's meaning, though there are also a number of continuities. Rituals for ensuring national prosperity and reverent veneration of the war dead remain alive in postwar Japan, for instance, both for some individuals and in certain religious institutions. Moreover, the framework of practical benefits provides another continuity of ritual's meaning before and after the war—at shrines and temples it is common to find people praying to *kami* (and *hotoke*) for both material and nonmaterial desirables (see Reader and Tanabe 1998).

The postwar shift in the official paradigm of ritual action did not lead to the production of value-free ritual practices.[17] Although different in character from the Ministry of Education's 1940 survey, for instance, many national surveys conducted after World War II by major newspapers sought to measure the level of Japan's "democratization" (Ishii 1997, 10). The 1946 survey conducted by the Ministry of Education was designed to measure people's "superstitious" tendencies in various parts of Japan (Meishin Chōsa Kyōgikai 1949, 5).[18] What the term "superstition" implied ranged widely from belief in the existence of ghosts, gods, monsters, and goblins to notions of luck, folk medicine, and spirit possession. Commenting on the published results of the 1946 survey, Education Minister Takase Shōtarō stated that people's superstitious tendencies tended to limit their lives (ibid., 1). Contradicting scientific thought and rational practice, superstitions were considered to hinder Japan's development as a cultured nation *(bunka kokka)*. Far from constituting objective measures of people's spontaneous thoughts, surveys were designed to judge, directly or indirectly, people's progress in accordance with certain values—the adoption of freedom of religion, for example, or a departure from superstition.

It is important to locate the declining number of believers in religion despite the persistence of ritual activity in postwar Japan, not only in the discourse of favoring "rational thought" as opposed to "superstitious" belief in certain supernatural entities, but also in postwar economic expansion and urbanization. When Nakada-*san* was in her thirties, an increased demand for labor in manufacturing and service industries encouraged the massive migration of rural populations to urban areas. The result was a rapid growth of urban populations often lacking strong ties with established channels for ritual activity, such as the neighborhood shrine venerating tutelary *kami* and family temples venerating ancestors (Fujii 1974; Ishii 1997, 97–98; Morioka 1970; Morioka and Hanajima 1968). Yet this did not lead to the disappearance of ritual activity. Some urbanites found new channels, while others utilized certain preexisting ones on a new scale or with a new twist. Granted full-fledged religious freedom, many new religious movements sprang up in postwar Japan, and some grew rapidly by providing channels for ritual activity to new urbanites (Tsushima 1992, 289), ranging from healing to ancestor veneration. Urbanites rediscovered renowned religious establishments in former capitals (Kamakura was one), and many prominent shrines and temples in cities became sites for mass-scale tourism and New Year visits during the 1960s (Murakami 1982, 106). Urbanization also encouraged the commercialization of certain life-cycle rites. During the 1970s, the number of funeral halls increased and offered commercialized funerals to new urbanites lacking solid community ties to conduct these rites (Suzuki 2000, 57). Commercialized wedding halls also sprung up to cater to people's needs (Edwards 1989). These trends of tourism and commercialization continued throughout the heyday of recent economic prosperity during the 1980s, known as The Bubble, and have not disappeared in today's long-term recession. As Japan underwent these changes in the political, economic, and social realms, the percentage of people surveyed who reported that they had religious beliefs declined from approximately half or two-thirds between 1946 and 1950 to some 30 percent between the early 1970s and 1980s.[19] The sarin attack of 1994 by the Aum Shinrikyō sect members is one notable incident in post-Bubble Japan that reportedly marked a further decline in the number of believers in religion to some 20 percent.[20] In this unprecedented crime, sect members randomly killed twenty-seven people and injured many more by releasing deadly poisonous gas on a Tokyo subway. (I began my fieldwork in the year after the gas attack.) Rituals in contemporary Kamakura, therefore, reside in complex historical and ideological contexts of today and recent past.

Thus, in her lifetime, Nakada-*san* saw a number of dramatic changes in the discourses of ritual action and the shifting channels of ritual activity in urban contexts. Despite some fluctuations, it was not until Nakada-*san* was in her late forties that we find 30 percent of believers in religion yet twice as many ritual actors, according to national surveys. And by the time she was in her early seventies, the number of believers had further declined to some 20 percent in some surveys. Yet, during these years, despite some fluctuations, national surveys tend to indicate no sharp decline in conventional ritual activities such as visits to ancestral graves and New Year visits to temples and shrines.[21]

Looking over this brief historical sketch, the gap that surveys reported between the number of ritual practitioners and believers in religion has not always been the defining characteristic of religion in Japan; surveys conducted in early postwar Japan indicate that the majority reported religion in which they believed. So we cannot assume that the small number of believers in religion reported in surveys derives from the pattern of ritual participation set in the Edo period (1603–1868), as some scholars have suggested (see, e.g., Kimura 2003). During the Edo period, families were required by the political authorities to participate in Buddhist rites to venerate ancestors, and the stem family *(ie)*, rather than the individual, was the unit of participation. Though historical practices do provide significant contexts for what happens today (see Chapter 1), discourses on religion and ritual in postwar Japan have undergone significant transformations despite certain continuities over time. Meanwhile, other scholars have reconsidered what "the number of believers" measures in the context of modernity and scrutinized the ways in which the notion of religion—a foreign, modern concept rooted in the Judeo-Christian tradition—became injected into and accommodated in the political discourse of the state (Shimazono 2004). Areligious or unreligious Japan, some argue, was created by Japan's accommodation of the belief-centered, foreign notion of religion (see, e.g., Yamaori 1996, 4–6).

While these perspectives stressing historical continuities and discontinuities are useful in illuminating ritual practice in today's Kamakura, this study will focus mainly on discovering situated accounts of ritual actions from the perspectives of ritual practitioners. By exploring ritual's meaning and relevance for those who maintain no strong commitment to religion, this ethnographic study will attempt to complement historical studies focusing on long-term change in ritual in modern Japan as well as surveys on ritual that provide large-scale trends at a national level.

Notes on Fieldwork

To understand how the meanings of ritual activity are (re)produced for the majority, I elected to concentrate not on a particular religious organization but on nonspecialists who are not particularly committed to any specific religion. Yet, it was not easy to obtain their perspectives. I did not have the founder of a religious organization or the author of a sacred text to whom I could turn. People I met in Kamakura were hesitant to discuss such issues as religious faith. Moreover, most people were reluctant to claim personal authority on ritual matters; they often thought it necessary to consult other sources of authority to explain rituals. Some referred to ethnological books about Kamakura; others suggested that I talk to a priest. In the case of neighborhood festivals, names of "elders" were cited as a source of information. A retired journalist in his early sixties who had written a memoir about neighborhood festivals and customs told me that people in Kamakura are already modernized. He said they no longer practice the "traditional" and "authentic" rituals described in ethnological works.

Yet my informants never referred to "the Japanese tradition" as a way of explaining what they did. Their response contrasts with the explanations an American colleague obtained when he studied Shinto rituals in southern Japan. When pressed by "why" questions, his informants reported: "We do this ritual because it is part of the Japanese tradition." My informants, on the other hand, cited certain aspects of the ritual that are unique to Kamakura or their own neighborhood. The only time I heard people explain their rituals by referring to "the Japanese tradition" was during the dedication of medieval archery at a shrine. Since the event attracts many tourists including foreigners, the announcement was made in English to cast it as truly traditionally Japanese.[22]

Despite people's reluctance, I kept asking for their personal views of ritual activity. Things began to go more easily when I began asking for explanations they might give to a child. I assumed that people wanted to teach children what is appropriate and important about ritual actions, and their explanations to them would likely contain what they considered to be significant. This approach evolved as I observed adults and children interacting with each other on ritual occasions during fieldwork. Furthermore, questions about movements, gestures, and place in ritual contexts often led to interesting discussions. Thus I began to focus on the meaning of certain gestures, movements, ritual objects, ritual sites, and placement of bodies and objects.

To be sure, I was including diverse populations and rituals in which people commonly participate. I talked to people of various ages, genders, and classes, and observed a range of rituals: domestic rites, visits to ancestral graves, life-cycle rites, festivals.[23] During fourteen months of fieldwork I attended more than eighty scheduled rituals, both Shinto and Buddhist, mostly public events in the oldest section of Kamakura City. When no rituals were scheduled, I visited workplaces and houses, conducted interviews, and observed people at Shinto shrines and Buddhist temples. At the end of my stay, I conducted a questionnaire survey about ritual life (N = 142).

I was an anomaly in the field—not because I look Japanese but am not, like American scholars of Japanese descent such as Hamabata (1990) and Kondo (1990), but because I did not fit into the life-course progression expected in Kamakura. Typically people there are expected to graduate from college, get a full-time job, marry, and have a family. These life phases tend not to overlap (Brinton 1992), particularly for women. Although women used to quit their full-time jobs when they got married, these days they are more likely to quit when they have children, and reenter the workforce—often as part-time employees—once their children are mature enough. I did not fit into this scheme. I was old enough to have a full-time job but didn't. And yet, unlike the typical student, I was not dependent on parents. In addition, I was old enough to have a family but lived alone. Furthermore, I often crossed lines of gender in male-centered networks of artisans and merchants. Since I was married, I did not have the experience of Matthews Hamabata (1990)—his informants tried to arrange a meeting with a prospective spouse.

Generally people treated me as not yet completely mature but beyond the immature stage of a dependent student. This depiction was partly strategic, because the largest initial problem I faced in the field was finding an entry into the community. Informants did not understand why I was interested in their everyday lives and what seemed trivial and obvious to them. In this my identity as a Japanese played a part—informants assumed that what they did would be self-evident to a Japanese person. My experience was very different from that of my American colleagues: they tend to stand out in Japan, and people usually assume foreigners need help. I, however, blended in quite well in Kamakura, a city that draws many tourists. To gain access to people and information, I needed to convey the idea that I needed explanations and introductions. My contacts with people in the initial stages of fieldwork, therefore, did not come as easily as they did for my American counterparts. Once I found a few people who were socially important and willing to give me introductions, though, fieldwork became efficient.

To protect the privacy of people who participated in this study, all informants' names in this book are pseudonyms. Place-names and attributes of some locations in Kamakura have also been changed.

Old Kamakura: The Site

Kamakura City, located at the southeastern end of Kanagawa Prefecture on Sagami Bay, is a city of 169,112 people (as of 1 March 2004) occupying 39.53 square kilometers (Figure 1). An hour away by train from Tokyo, Kamakura is an urban place with factories, commercial districts, family businesses, schools, hospitals, and modest farming and fishing populations. It is home to a diverse population typically found in urban communities elsewhere in Japan: white-collar workers, office clerks, civil servants, owners of small businesses, shopkeepers, housewives, students of different ages, children, and retired persons. Although Kamakura is urban, people often told me that it is "underdeveloped" (inaka) because it lacks the exciting nightlife and big commercial districts offered by major cities such as Tokyo and Osaka.

I conducted fieldwork in the district of Kamakura (Old Kamakura), one of the city's five. It is often assumed that people tend to be less concerned about social conventions, including ritual life, in urban areas. Yet despite its modern, urban lifestyle, Old Kamakura is known for a variety of ritual occasions. I therefore chose the district as a research site for a combination of reasons: its tradition of urbanism, residential stability, the presence of famous religious establishments, and frequent rituals and festivals.

Old Kamakura is best known to the public as a historic place because it was the capital during the Kamakura period (1185–1333).[24] The glory of Kamakura did not last long, however. It declined to the status of a provincial city during the Muromachi period (1333–1568) and was a little more than a collection of villages during the Edo (1603–1868). The town regained some of its prosperity when it became a prestigious resort for the national elites during the Meiji period (1868–1912).[25] This was a time when the construction of health resorts became popular, along with many other aspects of the West's material culture and customs. Later, as the transport system improved, Kamakura became a bedroom community of Tokyo and remains so to this day.

As elsewhere in Japan, whether people are employed or run their own businesses—and, in the case of employees, their company's size—shapes their identity in Old Kamakura. In general, white-collar employees of large corporations embody a new middle-class ideal; their positions are often considered more prestigious than those of the locally self-employed people *(jieigyō)* who run small family businesses, such as greengrocers, beauty-salon owners, electricians, and tea merchants.[26] Yet such ideas are often contested in multiple ways (Kondo 1990). Company employees, for example, are considered to have surrendered creativity and freedom in exchange for job security. The self-employed are

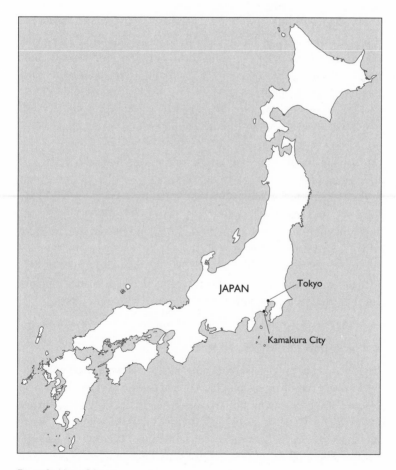

Figure 1. Map of Japan

considered freer and more independent, but their positions do have less prestige in mainstream society.

On a return visit to Kamakura in 2001, however, I discovered the waning prominence of white-collar employees in an economy in recession. Jobs at prestigious corporations are no longer assumed to be utterly secure, because the recession makes it difficult for these companies to ensure lifetime job security for all the regular (male) employees. Yet the situation for the self-employed is not significantly better, as the recession hit small-scale businesses even harder. During my return visit, an electrician who used to employ eight workers in 1996 told me that he now employs only two.

A person's work status is considered to manifest itself in attitudes, values, and lifestyles, including ritual life. The new middle-class people, for example, tend to be commuters who largely withdraw from community life; they leave Kamakura in the morning and come back in the evening. The old middle class, however, often live and tend their businesses in Kamakura. As a result, unlike the commuters, the locally self-employed are characterized by overlapping social, political, and economic networks. One person easily finds connections to another person through kinship ties, business ties, neighborhood ties, school ties, and friendship. Frequently I heard statements such as "Oh, he and I went to the same middle school," "Oh, she is my husband's relative," "My third son and her daughter were classmates," or "We're neighbors." Wives of commuters who came from Tokyo and moved to Kamakura when they married often described Kamakura as "narrow" *(semai)* because people tend to maintain such overlapping social networks. Due to their involvement in these networks, compared with salaried employees, self-employed people play a central role in community rites.

A Tour of Old Kamakura

Early on weekday mornings, commuters in formal dress arrive at Kamakura railway station by car, bus, bicycle, and on foot to get to their workplaces. During the day, particularly on weekends, flocks of tourists arrive at the station. Great waves of tourists visit during the seasons of cherry blossoms in April, hydrangea flowers in June, and fall leaves in November. Yet despite all the tourists, the city gains little economic benefit from its proximity to Tokyo, where most visitors stay.

At the left edge of Kamakura station's traffic circle, a torii gate indicates a beginning of a pathway leading to the renowned Tsuruoka Hachimangū Shrine (or just Hachimangū) via Komachi Street. The street is full of cafés and a variety of eating places offering full courses, lunch boxes, noodles, ice cream, and crepes. Tourists slowly zigzag down the street as they stop at fashionable boutiques, antique shops, china shops, and an incense store. Among the souvenir shops, a few stores for locals coexist, such as a tofu bean curd shop, beauty salons, bookstores, pharmacies, and an electric appliance store. Smells come from open-air stands baking rice crackers and steaming *omanjū* sweets.[27] Natives on bicycles skillfully navigate through the crowd. In spring and fall, groups of students on school trips, dressed in dark-blue uniforms, block the street as they walk in lines following their teachers.

Komachi Street brings a visitor to Hachimangū, the symbolic center of Kamakura. Originally built by the founder of the Kamakura shogunate, the shrine houses Hachiman-*sama,* protector of Kamakura's residents. Many tourists carry the dove-shaped cookies in bright-yellow paper bags decorated with the design of a large white dove—messenger of Hachiman-*sama.* Businesspeople are quick to employ symbols of Kamakura to their advantage. Hachimangū attracts a couple of million people every January, often ranking among the ten most popular sites for New Year visits in Japan. Wakamiya Ōji, the busiest main street, with its cars, bicycles, and pedestrians, connects Hachimangū and the beach areas in the south. Along the main street there are restaurants, groceries, bakeries, souvenir shops, a tatami-mat maker, a shoji-screen maker, a sword sharpener, sweetshops, a hospital, and a Catholic church.

Typically of Japan, Kamakura city consists of numerous neighborhoods *(chō),* and neighborhood associations act as semipublic institutions bridging residents and the municipal government. Old Kamakura is divided into eighteen neighborhoods, each of which is considered to have its distinctive characteristics. The neighborhood of Yuigahama along the beach, for example, used to be the center of prosperity during the resort era. Yet the popular and prosperous inns and hotels no longer exist; smaller residential homes have replaced them. On Yuigahama Street, a sweetshop occupies a Western-style concrete building that once impressed people with its modern appearance. With cracks in its wall, it no longer seems very modern. An old-fashioned fish store remains in business and is still known for its "second-home" price—the higher prices charged to wealthy vacationers with summerhouses during the resort era. I was told that this shop used to take orders from the house of the Nobel Prize–winning novelist Kawabata Yasunari. Descendants of summer vacationers, occupying much smaller lots they inherited, are scattered throughout the beach area. No longer a luxury limited to the nation's elite class, the beaches along Sagami Bay currently attract surfers and swimmers from late spring to early autumn. On weekends the bay, inundated with the colorful triangular sails of windsurfers, resembles a garden full of flowers. A small number of families still practice fishery in small boats, specializing in the aquaculture of seaweed and inshore fish. Early in the morning, older men and women can be seen collecting seaweed on the sandy beach.

In the late afternoon, the Kamakura station area bustles with housewives shopping for the evening meal. Large national-chain supermarkets stock regular, mass-produced foodstuffs, while Tokyo-based upscale supermarkets carry expensive imported food. Some of the small-scale, family-owned businesses deal in local products. Energetic shopkeepers quickly fillet and sell trays of shore fish. Farming women from neighboring communities bring their homegrown vegetables to the market. Local high school students stop at ice-cream stands or fast-food places like Kentucky Fried Chicken. On my recent visit to Kamakura in 2003, I discovered a Starbucks providing coffee lovers with an all-nonsmoking environment rarely found in Japan. The diversity of these businesses meets the needs of a diverse clientele.

By late evening, tourists are leaving and commuters are coming home. Most souvenir shops and restaurants close as soon as the tide of tourists begins to ebb, as early as six or so. At ten thirty in the evening, bus service ends for the day and gleaming black cabs take over the traffic roundabout. From a distance they resemble a school of black fish at the bottom of a dark ocean. Lighting up their headlights as commuters jump in, they disappear into the deep and quiet residential areas, away from the main streets. Although Kamakura's past makes it a unique place for residents, except for the presence of tourists in many respects the city looks just like other bedroom communities in Japan.

CHAPTER 1

Kami, Buddhas, and Ancestors

Although faith is not necessarily a primary reason for people to conduct rituals for *kami,* buddhas, and ancestors, the well-being of ritual practitioners and their families figures centrally as a motivation for ritual activity. On the one hand, people in Kamakura report a sense of obligation to participate in Shinto rituals at neighborhood shrines, or to venerate ancestors at home, because of their membership in family or community. In the case of motivated participation, on the other hand, a person conducts a ritual with certain hopes for benefits—for example, passing a college entrance exam, curing an illness, improving business conditions.[1] These two modes of ritual participation are not necessarily mutually exclusive, and the idea of well-being brings them together. Here I use the term "well-being" rather than "benefits," as the former is more widely used in social life, whereas the latter is associated mainly with religious worldviews and institutions. Focusing on both the unity and the diversity prevailing in ritual targets, occasions, ties, and places, this chapter will outline common patterns of ritual practice in Kamakura from a participant's perspective.

Ikeda-*san*'s Case

Ikeda-*san* is a woman in her late forties who runs an incense business. As an incense dealer and incense ceremony teacher, she constantly visits temples and travels frequently to major Japanese cities. Like many female friends her age, Ikeda-*san* takes ritual care of the *kamidana* (the altar to *kami*), a shelf made of plain white wood located near the ceiling in the family's gathering room. She offers a pair of evergreen branches *(sakaki)* to the altar on the first and the fifteenth days of the month.

Ikeda-*san* regularly offers cooked rice and green tea at the family altar, too, a small black lacquered box with built-in shelves. The altar accommodates the ancestral tablets of her great-grandparents-in-law, grandparents-in-law, parents-in-law, and her sister-in-law who died unmarried, but it lacks the tablets of her natal family members. Ikeda-*san* sends daily greetings to ancestors, seeking their protection of family members for the day. She also maintains a large family grave located at a renowned Zen temple near her house, although other family members—her husband, son, and daughter—also visit the grave to venerate the family dead. Three generations of her husband's ancestors rest in the grave, while ancestors from earlier times lie in a grave in Kyoto. The founding ancestor of Ikeda-*san*'s family was a famous medieval warrior, and maintaining the family's prestige adds greatly to the cost of tending graves.

Ikeda-*san* told me that she tends the domestic altars and the family grave because it is her responsibility as the matron of the conjugal family. In the Japanese stem family *(ie)*, most Japanese women leave their natal family and join their husband's when they marry. When Ikeda-*san* married, she joined the Ikeda family as a daughter-in-law, thus becoming a new member of her husband's stem family by taking his family name and coresiding with his parents. Her primary responsibility—ritual or otherwise—lies with this new family. When Ikeda-*san* dies, she will join the ancestors in the new stem family and ensure the well-being of her descendants. Although Ikeda-*san* does participate in ancestor rituals for the family dead in her natal family, it is the responsibility of the succeeding generation in her natal family—her eldest brother and his bride—to care for the natal family dead.

In addition to tending the domestic altars and the family grave, Ikeda-*san* routinely greets the tutelary *kami* venerated at the neighborhood shrine. On formal ceremonial occasions, she offers token gifts and petitions for the well-being of the family and for peace in the neighborhood. She also greets *kami* and buddhas at the shrines and temples she visits when she is traveling, although she is not so punctilious about these *kami* and buddhas.

When I asked Ikeda-*san* about her religion, she said she did not have one. She told me, "I have nothing to do with religion or the New Religions." This is a common response among my informants. Usually it means they do not belong to a religion that emphasizes personal faith, such as Christianity and the so-called New Religions. Ikeda-*san* says she does not have a personal interest in *kami* and buddhas or religious matters in general. She explained: "Before I got married, Shinto was my family's religion and *kami* were more important than they are now. At my natal home ancestors are enshrined at the *kamidana*.[2] At my marital home, however, ancestors are enshrined at the family altar."

Ikeda-*san*'s case illustrates many common features of people's ritual lives in Kamakura. For Ikeda-*san*—and for many other informants in Old Kamakura—ritual life is not so much about individual faith as it is about securing the well-being of their families and communities. It is common for people to maintain ties with several places enshrining *kami* and *hotoke*. Visiting such a place is not necessarily a consequence of membership in a particular religious establishment and adherence to its religious doctrine. Whether resulting from a sense of obligation or from a desire to obtain benefits, people's ritual lives are pervaded by a theme of seeking the well-being of participants and their companions. This contrasts with religions that emphasize individual faith, membership in a chosen congregation, weekly rituals at church, and exclusive commitment to a particular religious tradition.

Kami and *Hotoke*

As in other communities in Japan (Dore 1958; Guthrie 1988; Martinez 1995), *kami* and *hotoke* are the major foci of ritual attention in Old Kamakura. *Kami*, normally translated as "gods" or "deities," imply superhuman powers that control various forces such as rain, sun, poverty, and illness. Such powers may reside in nature, natural objects, domestic altars, yard shrines, small roadside shrines, major shrine establishments, and indeed in the living person. *Kami* have an authoritative dimension as well as humanlike, emotional aspects, as is evident in Japanese myths (Philippi 1968). Some *kami* are enshrined not only because they may be kind to their followers but also because they may harm people unless they receive ritual attention. People who have died tragic deaths, for example, may become vengeful *kami* known for their malicious influence on people.[3] Like *"kami,"* the term *"hotoke"* carries multiple meanings: the dead (either an individual or a collective), the enlightened, the founder of Buddhism (Buddha), Buddhist images, or someone exceptionally generous and honest (Umesao et al. 1995, 2020).

Despite these multiple meanings, Japanese people who are not ritual specialists commonly use *hotoke* to refer mainly to their family dead.

The relationship between *kami* and *hotoke* can best be characterized by their complementary coexistence. Although *kami* are mainly associated with Shinto and *hotoke* with Buddhism, people do not ordinarily question whether *kami* are more important than *hotoke*, or wonder whether they should be Buddhists rather than Shintoists. Shinto priests usually conduct life-cycle rites for the living, asking for *kami*'s help; Buddhist priests, in contrast, conduct rites for the family dead *(hotoke)*, asking for buddhas' help. *Kami* and *hotoke* are linguistically paired when someone regrets that "no *kami* or *hotoke* exists in the world" *(kami mo hotoke mo nai);* either they are both present or both absent. Furthermore, *kami* and *hotoke* are often enshrined at separate domestic altars in a single family home: *kami* protect the house and its residents; ancestors ensure the family's well-being. *Kami* and *hotoke* may even coexist within a single religious establishment. Buddhist temples in Kamakura often enshrine Buddhist images, their parishioners' ancestors, and the *kami* protecting their temple. A Zen priest in his forties explained, "*Kami* ensure the well-being of the places where buddhas are present, for Buddha cannot cover everything." This priest's view is not unusual. When I joined more than fifty Zen priests on a trip to Ise, they all visited the Ise Grand Shrines and had Shinto priests conduct a ritual for their prosperity.

Kami and ancestors are differentiated by the manners of greeting, offerings, and special ceremonial occasions, although the differentiation is not total. One is supposed to clap one's hands in front of *kami* and put one's hands together for *hotoke*. Yet, at shrines some visitors fail to greet *kami* in the Shinto manner with two bows, two claps, and one more bow. *Kami* like salty food offerings; *hotoke* like sweet ones (Cobbi 1995, 207). *Kami* are often offered raw food such as uncooked rice, raw fish, water, salt, and rice wine; *hotoke* frequently receive cooked food, cooked rice, tea, and sweets. Ancestors often receive individualized offerings such as cooked fish or even a chocolate cake—the foods they liked when they were alive (R. J. Smith 1974, 132). *Kami* are offered evergreen branches; *hotoke* are given incense. The distinction between *kami* and *hotoke*, however, is again less than total; fruits and rice cakes are offered to both. Ceremonially, ancestors become the center of ritual attention on the equinox days and on the Festival of the Dead in August; the *kamidana* becomes the center at the New Year—the time of renewal—although ancestors are honored as well (R. J. Smith 1974, 99). *Kami* and *hotoke* usually coexist without difficulty, yet when a death in the family occurs, a nonfamily member has to seal the *kamidana,* often with a piece of white paper. *Kami* are thought to loathe the state of ritual pollution caused by death.

People minimize differences between *kami* and *hotoke* by focusing on the parishioner's sincerity and thankful attitude. When Nomoto-*san,* the wife of a Buddhist priest, sent her eldest son to a Shinto kindergarten, a teacher asked her if it was suitable for him to be attending a Shinto kindergarten as he was to become the head priest of the Buddhist temple. Nomoto-*san* replied, "I told the teacher, 'When one prays sincerely, isn't one's heart *(kokoro)* the same whether facing *kami* or Buddha?'" Similarly, informants told me that to whom one is thankful—*kami* or *hotoke*—does not matter so much as one's gratitude. The idea of gratitude is deeply tied to the Japanese view that a person is fundamentally a social being with numerous links to both other humans and nonhumans.[4] A commonly used greeting, "I am indebted to you *(okage samade),*" acknowledges that one owes one's present success, or even one's state of being, to other persons, such as parents and superiors. People are who they are, not simply because they have worked hard or are talented, but because others have helped them—whether human or nonhuman benefactors. Not paying respect to *kami* and *hotoke,* therefore, could imply self-centeredness. A carpenter in his late fifties critically commented on his mother, who is famous for her bad temper, "She does not pay visits to temples and shrines; she thinks she is most respectable."

How Ritual Ties Are Organized

As in other long-standing communities in major Japanese cities, every two or three blocks a person visiting Old Kamakura will encounter a place enshrining *kami,* ancestors, and buddhas in the form of large Shinto and Buddhist establishments, neighborhood shrines, small communal roadside shrines, private yard shrines, and topographic sites such as sea and hill, without monuments or structures. Despite Japan's urbanization, technological accomplishments, and industrialization, these ritual places—places that enshrine *kami* and *hotoke*—coexist with urban life. There are more than 170 registered religious establishments in Kamakura and many that remain unregistered.

Despite its bewildering multiplicity at first glance, ritual life in Kamakura is well patterned according to kinship, territoriality, and specialized functions. The family altar and grave are defined by kinship: both enshrine ancestors. A variety of community shrines, defined by territoriality, protect inhabitants in various residential units. *Kami* are also enshrined to protect diverse places such as a company building, a restaurant, a boat, a community hall—even a baseball stadium. Meanwhile, some ritual places are defined primarily by their specialized powers: to cure illness, pass exams, assist in childbirth, advance one's business, ward off misfortune during years of calamity, find a spouse, and even help a person to die a swift and painless death in old age. However, the territorial, kinship, and functional ties defining ritual places are not mutually exclusive. For the parishioners of Hongakuji Temple, for example, the temple is the place where their ancestors are buried and venerated. Because the temple enshrines the Ebisu (*kami* of good business) in the temple compound, local merchants organize a territorially based festival. The Ebisu shrine also belongs to a pilgrimage route that attracts people participating in worship in more personal contexts. As a prayer temple, functional ties connect it and its followers, who attend monthly rituals to petition its founder for cures. Thus the elements of kinship, territoriality, and specialized functions intertwine to shape the temple as a ritual complex involving diverse functions and participants.

Although people in Old Kamakura come into contact with numerous ritual places, those defined by kinship and territoriality are often reported to be important.[5] As for places defined by kinship, 69 percent of the respondents in my survey reported that the family altar is important and 43 percent cited the family temple;[6] some 53 percent regarded the *kamidana* as important, 31 percent named the neighborhood shrine, and 30 percent cited the municipal shrine. It is worth noting that ties with ritual places that obligate people are especially valued. With the cultural logic of obligated participation, members of a stem family are under the protection of their ancestors, and residents of a neighborhood under the protection of the tutelary *kami*.

In contrast to ritual places defined by kinship and territory, ties with places defined by special functions tend to be personal and related to motivated participation. People more often brought up issues of the benefits and efficacy of their ritual acts when discussing these ritual practices. Baba-*san*, a woman in her late sixties, began regularly visiting the *kami* of learning at Egara Tenjin Shrine in Old Kamakura while her children were studying for their college entrance exams. Her children succeeded in their exams, so Baba-*san* then adopted the shrine for more general petitions regarding, for example, her children's health, safety, and happiness. Her tie with the shrine evolved from a temporary connection to a permanent one. On the other hand, a middle-aged informant explained that she never went back to a famous shrine in Tokyo known to help women avoid complicated childbirths because her petition had not been granted.

Caring for the *Kamidana*

Because obligated participation in rituals is based on a person's membership in a family and community, one might wonder if such practices are disappearing in a modern, urban context—could family and community ties be weakening? On the contrary, my study reveals persisting patterns of ownership and ritual care for domestic altars enshrining *kami* and ancestors in an urban setting. In Old Kamakura, the *kamidana* are frequently set up when a new house is built, a new office opens, or a family relocates (Figure 2). Newer houses, often equipped with carpeted rooms rather than formal, tatami-matted guest rooms, tend not to accommodate the *kamidana*. Some 55 percent of the seventy-four respondents in my Kamakura survey reported that they own altars to *kami*. Comparing these results with several postwar studies conducted during the 1950s and 1960s, the case of Kamakura indicates no sharp decline.[7] The figure for Kamakura in my survey (55 percent) is much higher than the average altar possession rate in Tokyo (30 percent) reported in the 1995 *Asahi Newspaper* survey (cited in Ishii 1997, 66).

The *kamidana* is commonly made of unfinished whitish wood in the shape of a miniature shrine with a roof and doors. Talismans are stored inside. The rope that hangs above the doors is ornamented with pieces of white paper indicating the purity of the place occupied by *kami*. Altars are equipped with a pair of vases, candle holders, and white dishes for offerings. A Shinto manual, *Shinto Manners and Knowledge* (Jinja Honchō 1995, 9), advises that every morning the head of the family or its representative should wash his/her face and rinse his/her mouth, change the water of the vase holding evergreen branches, light the candles at the altar, and make offerings (rice wine, water, salt, and washed rice). Yet my study indicates that only two-fifths of the altars receive daily offerings and greetings.[8] Three-quarters of the *kamidana* had only one caretaker. Although men and women are equally likely to greet *kami* at the domestic altar,[9] women are more frequently mentioned as caretakers in daily life and on special ritual occasions.[10] A forty-year-old business owner told me, "I do not know how often offerings are made to the *kamidana* at home, because my wife takes care of it." This statement contrasts sharply with the view expressed in the popular Shinto manual that the household head (usually male) is supposed to make offerings on behalf of his family.

Tending the Family Dead

As in other parts of Japan, in Kamakura the funeral is only the beginning of a long journey for the deceased on the road to achieving full-fledged ancestorhood: often they go through the first, third, seventh, thirteenth, seventeenth, twenty-third, twenty-seventh, and thirty-third memorial

Figure 2. The *Kamidana*

anniversaries. A woman at a Buddhist altar shop told me that prestigious families tend to observe the fiftieth and hundredth memorial anniversaries. By the end of the typical ritual cycle, the dead have left the memories of the living, as their contemporaries, one by one, have died out. Thus, the dead achieve stable ancestorhood by losing their personal characteristics (Plath 1964, 302).

The stem family locates people within the familial continuum consisting of generations of ancestors extending into future generations of descendants who are responsible for venerating ancestors. Consisting of a married couple and their unmarried children, the stem family, unlike the nuclear family, continues as long as a child remains in the family, takes a spouse, and produces the next generation (Brown 1966). The other siblings either join other stem families as in-marrying spouses or become the first generation of ancestors in new stem families by branching.[11] Following a typical Japanese pattern, the majority of families in Old Kamakura are affiliated with Buddhist temples. Buddhist priests who head these family temples conduct memorial and seasonal rites to venerate the family dead of parishioners. For my informants, the primary purpose of maintaining their parishioner status in family temples is to care for their ancestors.

In daily life, ancestors are permanently enshrined at the domestic altar while maintaining their social identity and participating in social life among the living. Ancestors are "fed" and "talked to"—they receive regular offerings and greetings. The family altar is often referred to by the kinship terms of the people enshrined there.[12] While ancestors provide a source of emotional attachment for family members, they also maintain authority over descendants by virtue of their seniority. Parents may scold children by saying, "What do your ancestors think of what you've done?" If the regular care given to the family dead implies expressions of respect and emotional attachment, the reverse is also true. Dorinne Kondo's informant, who married a patriarchal man in an arranged marriage, infrequently opens the Buddhist altar enshrining her late husband because she doesn't *want* to remember him (Kondo 1990, 133). She served her husband perfectly by taking care of all the housework and managing the finances, she explained; now she is a merry widow. Considering the fact that Japanese people have a fear of being ritually neglected and forgotten after death, which is regarded as a truly miserable condition, the widow has achieved her revenge by effectively cutting off her deceased husband from the daily social network and denying him the ritual care he expected to receive.

Ancestors are prayed to and prayed for (R. J. Smith 1974, 218): people ask (pray to) ancestors to ensure their well-being, but they also seek (pray for) their ancestors' peaceful rest. Whether people should petition ancestors—particularly regarding problematic issues—is a matter for discussion.[13] Problem-oriented petitions are made to resolve specific issues such as finding a marital partner or passing a college entrance exam. At the family grave, informants tend to make generalized petitions rather than problem-oriented pleas. Imai-*san,* a woman in her late forties, told me that she corrected her teenaged daughter when she voiced problem-oriented petitions at their family grave. Yet when an electrician's son was about to take a college entrance examination, he told me that he petitioned his father at his family grave. When I pointed out that people commonly visit Shinto shrines, not the family grave, to ask for their success in entrance examinations, he told me: "Normally I don't visit my father's grave for petitions at all. Yet it occurred to me to do so this time." Thus although ancestors are usually asked to secure general well-being for their descendants, occasionally they function in a way similar to *kami* and buddhas—they are thought to be able to help descendants achieve specific goals.

As a symbol of the family (Plath 1964), ancestors may also be mobilized in a family dispute. Matthews Hamabata's informant's aunt, Otoyo, removed untended ancestral tablets from the empty house of a former household head in order to provide them with proper ritual care in her home (Hamabata 1990). The matter was complex, however, because there were two eldest sons in the Itō family, one by their father's first wife, and another by his second; Otoyo is the wife of the eldest son by the first wife. Coming from a lower socioeconomic background, Otoyo was scorned and bullied by the women in this renowned business family. They became furious when Otoyo "stole" the tablets—"the heart and soul of the family"—but could not challenge her publicly because she was fulfilling her filial duty as the eldest son's wife (Hamabata 1990, 112). Conventionally it is the right and the duty of the household head and his wife to care for ancestors. By making a place for the ancestral tablets in her home, Otoyo lay claim to her husband's legitimacy as the successor and hers as the successor's wife in the context of a succession dispute and consequent turmoil. Places enshrining ancestors, therefore, can be used in family politics—to define, contest, or legitimate the boundaries of the family and its members' status.

Caring for the Family Altar

Unlike altars to *kami,* family altars tend to be dark-colored, commonly made of black lacquered wood decorated with shiny, golden metal (Figure 3). Although expensive altars may cost tens of thousands of dollars, a small apartment-sized altar can be found in shopping catalogs for about two hundred dollars. Behind its doors, the family altar commonly holds the principal Buddhist image, ancestral tablets, pictures of the recent dead, and ritual utensils such as lanterns, rice dishes, tea containers, vases, offering trays, an incense bowl, and a candle holder. In a drawer, people often keep amulets, passbooks, seals, sutra books, and a booklet containing the names of the family dead. Ancestral tablets are typically made of black lacquered wood inscribed with the posthumous names of the dead. A low table is placed in front of the altar for a bell, a striker, and an incense holder. Though Buddhist manuals often advise that the family altar is a place to enshrine buddhas and say that it can

Figure 3. Family Altar for Ancestors

be set up anytime, informants define the altar as the place to enshrine ancestors.

According to my study, 74 percent of the respondents said they own family altars. The figures for altar ownership were 80 percent in a Tokyo neighborhood in 1951 (Dore 1958); 63 percent in Tokyo in 1955 (cited in R. J. Smith 1974, 88); 69 percent among blue-collar residents in Tokyo, 45 percent among white-collar residents in Tokyo, and 92 percent in an agricultural village in Yamanashi Prefecture between 1964 and 1965 (Morioka 1970, 153). But why is the altar possession rate among white-collar residents in Tokyo so much lower (45 percent) than that in Kamakura (74 percent)? Kamakura's altar possession rate can be explained by considering the formation cycle of the stem family and urbanization. The city experienced rapid urbanization during the 1950s and 1960s. Then the population increase slowed down. Currently the city is residentially stable, and many of the newer branch families that moved to Kamakura during the 1950s and 1960s have already experienced deaths in the family. An altar is usually set up when a death occurs in the stem family; newly founded branch families tend to lack family altars in their homes. Thus in expanding urban communities in Tokyo in the 1960s, many new branch families did not own family altars because there were no deaths in the stem family. Furthermore, the altar possession rate in Kamakura is even higher than the national average (59 percent) based on a survey conducted by *Asahi Newspaper* in 1995 (cited in Ishii 1997, 66). Certainly ancestors have not disappeared from city life.

When greeting ancestors at the family altar, one sits formally on the floor with legs folded, lights a candle and a long incense stick, and places the stick in the incense bowl. Then one rings the chime to beckon the ancestors and puts one's hands together to pray. Only a few people said they chant sutras. Some 71 percent of the altar owners in my survey said they greet their ancestors at the family altar every day.[14] According to Robert Smith's survey conducted in 1963, some 62 percent of ancestral tablet owners reported that they participate in the daily morning rites— greeting ancestors and offering freshly cooked food (R. J. Smith 1974, 105). Similarly, 64 percent of the respondents in Kamakura said that they make daily offerings, such as green tea and freshly cooked rice.[15] When pressed, however, my informants told me they offer rice whenever it happens to be cooked—ancestors sometimes have to wait until lunch or dinnertime, when rice is ready. Many Japanese people today eat bread instead of freshly cooked rice for breakfast, and offerings are changing as lifestyles change. During a field trip to Tokyo in 1998, a salesperson at a "new-style" family altar shop told me that one of her customers offers a cup of coffee and a piece of toast to her deceased husband every morning—what he used to eat for breakfast.[16]

Unlike caregiving activities for the altar to *kami*, making daily offerings to the family altar is a communal act that involves several family members.[17] Although there are no clear gender differences regarding the ritual greeting to ancestors at home,[18] women are more often mentioned as caretakers of the family altar on ritual occasions, both regular and special.[19] For regular offerings, men are frequently listed along with female members of the family such as their wives and mothers. Although women usually regard regular caretaking activities for home altars to be part of their domestic responsibilities, men are not excluded from tending these altars. Nor are women excluded from the formal ritual occasions surrounding domestic altars, such as death anniversaries, the New Year celebrations, equinoxes, and the Festival of the Dead (cf. Kendall 1985, 170–171; Sered 1999). My informants rarely cited gender as preventing men or women from deviating from the common patterns of ritual care for domestic altars.

The Family Grave

While the family altar is considered to house ancestors within a family home, the family grave is treated as a house for ancestors in the outside world (Figure 4). A woman who married a Buddhist priest told me: "I always had a sense that, at the family grave, I could see my mother, who died young." Although some people visit their graves once a month or more frequently, most residents of Old Kamakura visit their family graves on the annual death days, two equinoxes, the Festival of the Dead in August, and the New Year. People in other parts of Japan often follow this pattern, too, except for the New Year. Seasonal rites for the dead are commonly held at family temples on equinoxes and during the Festival of the Dead in summer.

One hot afternoon, I witnessed a summer veneration ritual *(segaki)* at my landlady's family temple in Kamakura. To the sound of bells and a wooden drum, Zen priests, dressed formally in dark-colored layered clothes, chanted sutras in unison. The priests then burned incense at the altar, which held a large black tablet representing the parishioners' family dead. Facing a portable incense table, my landlady raised her right hand grasping a small amount of incense and released it into a bowl to venerate her ancestors. Then parishioners fed the pitiable hungry ghosts at a separate altar located at the edge of the ritual hall. After the veneration ritual, parishioners received long, thin pieces of wood bearing the donors' names and prayers and then visited their family graves, located behind the temple. The temple cemetery was crowded with rectangular gravestones supported by two square layers of stone at the bottom. People washed the gravestone, burned incense, and made offerings such as flowers, foods, and drink to the ancestors. While the majority of the graves received washing, flowers, and offerings, some were deserted. Without descendants to care for them, the dead in untended graves are destined to become pitiable, homeless souls *(muenbotoke)*.

Tending the family dead properly is a moral act that embodies a person's commitment to the stem family. Consider, for example, the case of Machida-*san,* a woman in her late forties. Her brother-in-law (her husband's elder brother) and his wife became Christians in their fifties and began to set themselves apart from their relatives. When Machida-*san*'s parents-in-law died recently, the descendants had to choose the suc-

Figure 4. Family Graves

cessor to their family grave, usually inherited by the eldest son.[20] Her brother-in-law wanted to put a cross on the gravestone. Both she and her husband disagreed strongly with this proposal because their family religion is the Nichiren-*shū* of Buddhism. Machida-*san*'s husband told his brother that he and his wife could purchase a new, Christian-style grave for themselves. The eldest brother rejected this idea, however, for this would imply a loss of his conventional right as the eldest son. Since the eldest brother is the trustee, not the owner, of the family grave, Machida-*san* and her husband contested the status of the successor—the eldest son—based on the cultural logic that the successor should ensure the well-being of ancestors. In Machida-*san*'s view, her husband's older brother had implied that he would "convert" his ancestors to Christianity by placing a cross on the family gravestone, and this was considered a legitimate reason for the second son and his wife to question the eldest son's fitness as guardian of the family grave and tradition. Their intervention prevented the modification of the familial gravestone—at least for the moment. Ancestors continue to symbolize the family in Kamakura.

A Historical Sketch

Although even a brief outline of Japan's religious history is beyond the scope of this chapter, it is worth stressing that past religious policies have played a significant role in shaping the present conventions—in particular, obligatory ties defined by kinship and territoriality. In the past, nationwide regulations encouraged the installation of domestic altars and affiliation with Buddhist temples and local Shinto shrines. During the Edo period (1603–1868), the Tokugawa shogunate required everyone to register at a Buddhist temple and practice ancestor veneration (the *terauke* system). The temples maintained a religious register recording the members of the household and their family temple, their Buddhist school of affiliation, their place of birth, and their current address. The practice of religious registry spread nationally around 1660 and indeed came to serve as a census (Tamamuro 1971, 81). This obligatory affiliation with Buddhist temples was intended to suppress Christianity, which was forbidden by the shogunate. Since Christianity placed one's relationship to God first, it was considered a threat to the social foundation of Japan, with its stress on loyalty to the feudal lords and the shogunate. In the *terauke* system, Buddhist temples gained the authority to verify that their parishioners were not Christians by performing Buddhist ancestral rituals for them.

Although the *terauke* system has been abolished, people today conventionally maintain their affiliation with Buddhist temples in order to venerate the family dead. Just as ritual actors during the Edo period demonstrated that they were not Christians by using Buddhist veneration rites, so people today use the term *"mushūkyō"* (having no religion) for a similar purpose. The word implies that a person does not belong to any religion that emphasizes personal faith, such as Christianity or the so-called New Religions. *Mushūkyō* persons often follow social convention by participating in life-cycle and calendrical rites at Shinto shrines and Buddhist temples. Thus the state of "having no religion" is far from atheism but implicitly denies what a person is not.

Just as political leaders used the family altar and the family temple during the Tokugawa period, the prewar state authorities used altars to *kami* and the community shrines as political tools. The Meiji Restoration in 1868 marked the end of the long-lived Tokugawa shogunate and its hegemony; the emperor regained political leadership. Under the leadership of the lower-class samurai warriors from the former Satsuma and Chōshū domains, a new centralized government was established. This new government empowered Shinto—long subordinated under Buddhism—and developed State Shinto as the national ideology, thereby strategically diminishing the Buddhist influence from the previous Tokugawa period. In order to legitimate the authority of the imperial system and the new state, the Meiji government passed a series of laws in 1868 officially separating Shinto and Buddhism. This measure ended long-standing efforts by previous political leaders to blend the two. Thereafter all Buddhist buildings, images, and objects were removed from shrine-temple complexes.

The Meiji government also encouraged the already widespread placement of altars to *kami* in homes and nationalized the distribution of Ise talismans representing the ancestral *kami* of the imperial family. Under the new state, Shinto priests became national servants and "encouraged people to acquire and maintain domestic altars, to place Ise talismans in them as an object of worship, and to perform obeisance before the altar daily" (Hardacre 1989, 87). While the altar to *kami* was designated the central ritual site within the household, the Meiji government also used village and neighborhood shrines for the propagation of the national ideology in a community setting. Meiji policies encouraged the alignment of administrative territories (village, town) and shrine territories. Local shrines became ritual centers to unite several smaller territorial units *(aza)* and consolidate new administrative towns and villages (Morioka 1987). The state stipulated that every subject must become a parishioner of a territorially defined shrine; affiliation with a shrine was obligatory and based on the household. The Meiji government also abolished the temple registration system and attempted to use local Shinto shrines for population registry. Yet the family registration system based on local shrines was soon discontinued; it was replaced by the national family register system in 1871. Today the state no longer uses neighborhood shrines for population registry, nor are they officially connected to municipal administrative units. Nonetheless, the idea that the neighborhood shrine protects those who live in the vicinity—regardless of their personal religious faith—is not uncommon among residents of Kamakura and in Japan at large, particularly among older people, natives, and local businesspeople.

The family's continuing possession and caretaking of domestic altars and the family grave indicate that these ritual practices have survived urbanization and are part of fully modern, changing lifestyles in Japanese society today. Although to different degrees, people in Kamakura recognize a sense of obligation to conduct rituals at domestic altars, community shrines, and family graves, and these places are valued more highly than others. Historically, these patterns of ritual activity that survive in Kamakura today owe much to former religious policies. Nonetheless, many other practices that were imposed upon people in the past have disappeared. Former religious dictates certainly created the context for practices today, but they alone cannot explain people's present experiences and the future of these practices.

CHAPTER 2

Embodying Moral Order

Acting Bodies and the Power of Ritual

Japan's Ministry of Foreign Affairs (1999) maintains a web page that introduces various aspects of Japanese culture in English. In its intriguing introduction about Shinto, an explanation states: "the absence of official sacred scriptures in Shinto reflects the religion's lack of moral commandments. Instead, Shinto emphasizes ritual purity and cleanliness in one's dealings with the *kami*." The web page explains that, as a leading publisher (Kōdansha International) prepared the introduction, it "does not necessarily reflect the opinions of the ministry." Nevertheless, the statement exposes a covert assumption that in an English-speaking society a primary function of religion is to provide a code of ethics—and Shinto does not fit into this picture. This view is consistent with an anecdote related by a colleague of mine. When he was a beginning graduate student in a leading philosophy department at an American university, he informed an ethics professor of his plans to study ethical systems in East Asian cultures. The professor's discouraging response was that no such systems exist.

Ancestor worship, another major facet of religious expressions in Japan, is clearly connected to morality: ancestors represent a source of conscience for people (Plath 1964, 307). Children may be scolded and warned that their conduct might make their ancestors sorry. Nonetheless, morality is not the central theme in anthropological studies of Japanese ritual, which often highlight social structures, community boundaries, and social identities that are contested or strengthened through ritual activity (cf. Bestor 1989; Martinez 1998; Ohnuki-Tierney 1987; Ooms 1967; Robertson 1991; Schnell 1999; Suzuki 2000).[1]

True, as the Ministry of Foreign Affairs' web page maintains, Shinto does lack sacred texts that provide a moral code of conduct in written form. Although Buddhists maintain sacred texts, most people—excluding scholars, priests, and the religiously committed—do not read them, nor do they try to understand them. Some people learn to chant sutras in classical Chinese, but they often do so without knowing precisely what the sutras mean. Yet studying written ethical codes is not the only way to address moral concerns. Nor is morality always expressed in terms of the conduct of an individual cut off from the rest of society.

An article, titled "Old Accident Points to Brain's Moral Center" from the *New York Times* (24 May 1944; cited in Howell 1997, 1), reveals a number of assumptions behind the notion of morality in Western thought. The story describes the personality change of a railroad man who survived brain damage in an accident. According to the story, the man could make rational decisions but not moral ones. A philosopher and a cognitive scientist studied the matter and concluded that the man's moral core in his brain, which allowed him to make moral decisions, had been injured in the accident. Commenting on this story, Signe Howell (1997, 1) points out that this conclusion "reflects a long-standing tradition within Western academic discourse to make claims concerning human nature from within some kind of natural science mode." This story also reveals a cultural conception that morality is contained in a person's head.

Japanese expressions of moral value, in contrast, often center on ideas of interpersonal hierarchy as well as mutual dependence. Indebted feelings toward ancestors, parents (DeVos 1986, 84, 97), and others define a person's sense of moral duty.[2] In other words, proper social relations themselves constitute and express moral order. And rather than becoming externalized as codes or being located in one's head, mind, or thought, these moral ideas often find expression in the acting bodies and their functions and states. In contrast to the medical and biological concept of menopause that exists among North American women, for example, in Japanese settings the intense physical discomfort associated with menopause is believed to indicate a woman's lack of "moral fiber" (Lock 1993). Morally strong women are expected to have an easy ride through menopause. The body, therefore, is much more than a biological entity; it is also a social entity whose conditions are morally defined.

Due to its moral relevance, the body becomes the site for disciplining and producing moral selves. In contrast to the Western mind/body dichotomy that encourages the separation of self from body, a common Japanese pedagogy discourages this split. Dorinne Kondo's accounts (1990) of an "ethics retreat" to produce ideal workers vividly delineate the ways in which physical forms of discipline—cleaning, exercising, running a marathon, greeting, sitting on the ground, bathing in cold water—are meant to discipline not only the body itself but also the *kokoro:* the mind and the heart of participants. In other words, the form of action imposed on the body is thought to have the power to transform the inner self. For this reason, such disciplines are commonly found in Japanese workplaces and educational institutions (Ben-Ari 1997; Benjamin 1997).

Extending this line of thinking, I shall now examine meanings of common ritual activity in Kamakura—both Shinto and Buddhist—and explore their moral relevance. My definition of morality is broader than the notion of "Ethics Narrow," which focuses on the individual's obligation or duty, discussed in the book *Anthropology and Ethics* (Edel and Edel 1959, 9). I focus on character—what a good person is expected to do in relation to others and one's surroundings and, moreover, the kinds of violations that cause people to question someone's character.

Because moral ideas are often expressed in bodily terms in daily life, to understand the ritual lives of Japanese informants we need to examine not only belief—the cognitive aspects—but also practice, especially bodily actions (cf. Bell 1992; Csordas 1994b; Sullivan 1990). What kinds of bodily actions or movements *(dōsa)* do people commonly use in their ritual lives, and what are their meanings? How do these bodily actions enhance the power of ritual? The analysis presented here reveals two kinds of ritual activity commonly used in Kamakura: key ritual actions and restricting ritual actions. Key ritual actions are an aggregate of bodily actions and practices commonly found in both ritual and everyday contexts. Restricting ritual actions, on the other hand, are bodily practices primarily found in ritual contexts but rare in everyday life.

Key Ritual Actions

Several years ago, I was watching a Japanese drama titled *Doku* about students from different parts of Asia studying Japanese. Although these students from Vietnam, China, and Korea were supposedly studying ele-

mentary Japanese, during emotionally intense scenes, the students acting the drama apologized, thanked, or showed respect by bowing in
different ways. Thus they communicated in a culturally sophisticated
manner, through silence and bowing, subtle behavior I generally expect
from native speakers. The screenwriter should have realized that bodily
communication results only from intense socialization in a culture.

Bowing

Common ritual actions in Kamakura, such as bowing, are often
central social acts with moral significance. Japanese people bow when
greeting each other, showing respect, being polite, thanking, asking a
favor, or apologizing. Many books on manners show the proper ways of
bowing at different levels of formality. The most formal bow requires
one to lower the head and upper body to form a ninety-degree angle,
whereas a less formal bow requires just a sixty-degree angle. When a person is seated on the floor with legs folded, a deep bow requires that the
forehead touch the floor. A fifty-nine-year-old sweets merchant summarized the function of bowing neatly: "Bowing is proper manners for
everything."

Bowing to *kami* and ancestors is performed for reasons similar to
those in everyday life—to greet, show respect, thank, ask for a favor.[3]
Both Shinto and Buddhist rites involve frequent bowing. The main portion of a Shinto rite usually begins and ends with a deep, formal bow by
the head priest. When a Shinto priest opens the door of a shrine and
another priest calls "Ō . . . ō . . . ō . . ." to signal the descent of *kami*, all
the participants lower their heads to show respect. Similarly, when the
head priest performs the most formal bows to Buddha, he generally
kneels on a cloth spread on the ground and repeats the deep bows by
bringing his head down to the ground. When Buddhist priests utter
words to distribute the benefits of chanting to the parishioners, they put
their hands together and bow deeply. During seasonal ancestral rites
held at a Buddhist temple, parishioners go to the altar, where they bow,
put their hands together, and burn incense to venerate the family dead;
here, bowing is performed to show gratitude and respect and to ensure
the well-being of the family dead. In short, the act of bowing in both ritual and everyday contexts embodies the thankfulness and respect considered indispensable to Japanese social relations.

Cleaning

Cleaning, like bowing, is an act filled with moral meaning. It involves not only practical value but also the moral value of purity.[4] Thus cleaning is not always relegated to a specialized occupational group. The entranceway of a house is swept regularly. People take their shoes off at the entrance to prevent tracking dirt into the house. Employees of a shop begin and end their workday with cleaning. Grade school students learn to clean their own classrooms. Since cleaning is not simply performed for the sake of hygiene but is considered to better the inner self, it constitutes a form of moral discipline in a variety of contexts: in religious institutions such as Zen temples (Reader 1995), in the utopian religious movement known as Ittōen (Davis 1975, 292), in the ethics retreat (Kondo 1990), in the workplace, and in the classroom (Benjamin 1997).

Women are often the central actors in maintaining cleanliness in homes and offices. Many Japanese housewives report that they frequently clean their houses. Young female workers are often required to clean their office before work begins; they have to arrive at their workplace earlier than the male workers in order to wipe the desks with wet cloths and so on. Just as it is essential to have a clean house, it is good to keep the family grave tidy so that ancestors will feel comfortable. Indeed, women often expressed their concern about tending the family grave and domestic altar.

At a Shinto shrine, cleaning becomes a ritual directed to *kami* at the end of the year. Priests and staff of all ranks participate in this rite by dusting the ceiling, washing sliding windows, and wiping down the surface of the building. This year-end cleaning takes place not only at shrines but also at homes, shops, companies, and temples. Cleaning is a culturally valued act of preserving or restoring order in domestic and ritual places.

Purification

Along with bowing and cleaning, purification is another key ritual act that is morally significant in daily life. Purification is tied to boundaries: the gateways of a place and the gates of the body are major targets of purification (cf. Douglas 1966, 126). People maintain the purity of their bodies, for example, by washing their hands and gargling when they come home. After sweeping, water is poured onto the sidewalks, particularly during the hot summer months.

In addition to defending gateways, people maintain purity by keeping the proper order in bodily and spatial terms. Bodies and places have qualitatively different portions consisting of "high" and "low," "front" and "back," "exterior" and "interior" parts. (For a detailed discussion, see Chapter 3.) Objects that belong to "high" portions of the house and the body should not be mixed with those belonging to "low" parts. For example, people should never wipe the dining-room table with rags used for washing the floor; because they are used to clean the "lower" part of the house, they are not pure enough to clean the table. Similarly, people should never wear slippers used in the bathroom in other parts of the house; otherwise, the dirt associated with toilets would travel all over the house. Shinoda-*san*, a woman in her forties, told me that she was shocked when she saw her American friend place a pair of high heels on top of her new dress when packing her suitcase: "I told my friend to put the shoes in a bag. She said that since the shoes weren't really dirty, it was OK." Shinoda-*san* told me that her friend had missed the point—shoes and clothes should never be mixed together. In her view, shoes belong to the "low" area since they touch dirt on the ground, whereas clothes do not. Strict separation of "high" and "low," therefore, creates a sense of order by preventing contamination of pure objects, body parts, or areas of the house. Furthermore, dirty things are not purely "mental" phenomena. They are embodied and emplaced—and are therefore deeply experiential (cf. Douglas 1966).

Kami, like the Japanese people themselves, are known for their love of purity. Shinto shrines are equipped with stone sinks where visitors wash their hands and rinse their mouth, as they must purify themselves before encountering *kami.* Similarly, one should wash one's face and hands and rinse one's mouth before performing regular morning greetings to *kami* enshrined at the domestic altar. In Shinto rites, a variety of purification techniques and agents are used: pouring water, bathing in the sea, spreading hemp, rubbing with paper, shooting arrows, ringing bells. During a ritual dance *(kagura)* dedicated to *kami,* the dancing priest dips bamboo branches into a mixture of boiling water and rice wine and then splashes the participants and the shrine compound. This rite drives away evil and keeps those who are splashed healthy. During the rite of great purification, pieces of hemp are sprinkled over the parishioner's head to wash away ritual pollution. Participants breathe on pieces of paper shaped in the form of people and then rub their bodies with these pieces to restore their purity. Priests then collect the pieces of paper and throw them into the bay.

Although purification is more immediately associated with Shinto than with Buddhism, Buddhist rituals do employ purification techniques. Followers of Myōō-in Temple, for example, rub afflicted areas of their bodies with wooden sticks at a monthly festival. A middle-aged woman next to me told her son, "Rub your head to make yourself smarter!" The negative elements—such as pain and stupidity—are transferred onto wooden sticks, which are then ritually burned by Buddhist priests.

Ancestors, too, value purity. Even if the grave is not dirty, people may wash it and pour water over the gravestone to beautify and purify. When caretakers wash the grave and water the gravestone during the Festival of the Dead, it is seen as cooling off and refreshing the ancestors on a hot summer day. A twenty-eight-year-old graduate student went even further: to pour water onto the gravestone, she said, means to bathe one's ancestors. Japanese people are known for their love of bathing, not solely for hygienic cleanliness but also for purity, relaxation, and pleasure (Clark 1994). Pouring water onto the gravestone may give ancestors a similar good feeling. In addition to defending boundaries of territories, therefore, acts of purification create the culturally valued condition of purity in mundane and ceremonial contexts alike.

Offering and Sharing

In addition to bowing, cleaning, and purification, the acts of offering and sharing are deeply tied to the moral idea of mutual dependence and reciprocity. The act of offering is thought to embody the quality of relationships between persons as well as among people, *kami,* and *hotoke.* When visiting Shinto shrines or Buddhist temples, some people offer money to *kami* and buddhas as a thank-you gift for having been granted specific petitions or provided general protection. Others give money in exchange for a favor. Yet Shinto shrines carefully emphasize that the money is an offering, not a payment; shrines frame exchanges between people and *kami* outside the world of commercial transactions. For example, shrines do not "sell" amulets, rather they "let people reverently receive" amulets *(sazukeru).* Similarly, when I thought I had bought two books at a stand in the shrine compound, my receipt stated "as a donation to the shrine," even though I had had no intention of making an explicit donation. Whether it is a form of payment or not, the act of offering sustains people's ties with *kami,* buddhas, and ancestors. An informant in her eighties told me that she makes donations to show gratitude. Behind the act of offering is a sense that one's life is not completely one's own but instead is sustained by those beyond oneself, whether *kami* or human superiors. As my informants occasionally told me, people do not simply live, they are "allowed to live" by forces beyond themselves, and thus are indebted to others for their existence. The act of offering, therefore, expresses such a sense of indebtedness.

The act of offering also embodies the Japanese value of connectedness. As Japanese people are fundamentally constituted by their links with others, it is important to have good connections in order to live a happy life. "Good connections" often refers to finding a spouse, since marriage binds two families together. The phrase for "no connection" *(en ga nai)* essentially means that one is unfortunately single. Similarly, the dead who are unfortunately childless (and hence are not venerated correctly) become "the disconnected dead" *(muenbotoke)*—that is, "disconnected," with no links to the chain of generational continuity in the family. People commonly give five yen as a token donation at shrines and temples so that they will form many connections. (Phonetically, "five yen" is read *"goen,"* a homonym for the term "connection.") Since having good connections cannot be achieved simply through one's effort or goodwill, *kami* and *hotoke* are asked to help with this unpredictability.

In explaining the practice of offering in a ritual context, informants drew from their experiences of gift giving and sharing. In Kamakura as well as other parts of Japan, gifts are given on formal and informal occasions to thank, to ask a favor, to send greetings, to celebrate, and to express concern in times of crisis. In June and July as well as December, department stores set up special sections displaying a variety of packages for calendrical gift-giving seasons—consisting predominantly of items for consumption such as food, drink, and household articles. During the New Year holidays, people give gifts to renew ties with friends, family, colleagues, and clients. Celebratory gifts are given for births, life-cycle rites for three-, five-, and seven-year-olds *(shichigosan),* coming of age *(seijin shiki),* entrance to and graduation from school, and birthdays. Gifts are also given on inauspicious occasions such as funerals, memorial anniversaries, hospitalization, accidents, or natural disasters. Gifts are not limited to material goods; they may include a variety of intangibles such as time, effort, attention, or care. Some gifts require gifts in return fairly swiftly; others may be paid back after a long interval— even a generation, for example, in the case of caregiving to aging parents (Hashimoto 1996). Furthermore, those with skills in gift giving are admired and appreciated; those without these skills risk getting a reputation of questionable character. Harumi Befu (1986, 163) makes a similar point about gift-giving skills and their moral relevance in rural Japan. If a person gives a gift that is much cheaper than one is expected to give, "people will gossip about the cheapness not only of the gift but also of the giver's character." Despite the urban lifestyle of its residents, this is also the case in Kamakura.

The sharing of food and drink is another essential act in Japanese social life that contributes to establishing and maintaining the valued idea of connectedness between persons (Befu 1974; Ohnuki-Tierney 1993). Among male informants, drinking beer or rice wine together is a common way to get to know their coworkers. Not only is it considered rude to serve yourself alcohol, but pouring each others' drinks is a way of maintaining social connections. On a trip I took with Buddhist priests and employees of a Zen temple, my key informant went through every row of seats in a banquet room exchanging drinks and greetings.[5] As this custom of exchanging endless drinks could often lead to the production of unintelligible fieldnotes, I quickly learned to take symbolic sips on these occasions.

Just as people sustain themselves through gift giving, so the act of offering sustains people's connections with ancestors, buddhas, and *kami*. Offering food, drink, and flowers to *kami* and *hotoke* is often explained by referring to the gifts given in everyday life. Just as guests are entertained by banquets, *kami* and *hotoke* receive food and drink at home and at religious establishments. People explained that they offer flowers as a decoration at the family grave to make ancestors' houses beautiful.[6] The sharing of food and drink is also a way of strengthening connections between people and targets of ritual attention. After a Shinto ritual, the rice wine dedicated to *kami* is shared among ritual participants. Sometimes a separate meal is prepared for participants to receive "leftover" offerings from *kami*. When I attended an annual festival of Daikoku-*sama* (the *kami* of fortune), the caretaker gave me a portion of the offering, a sweet red-bean cake. Sharing offerings also occurs as a daily routine. When people make a new rice offering to ancestors, they remove the old offering and add it to the rice cooker for sharing. By regularly sharing rice—the staple food—ancestors and descendants maintain their connections. Thus the acts of offering and sharing forge and reforge valued links among humans, *kami,* and *hotoke.*

Embodying Values

Considering that explanations for key ritual actions are not routinely discussed, theorized about, or explicitly taught, a surprising regularity is found regarding their meaning. Essentially informants draw meaning from their everyday experiences. A close examination of these acts reveals an array of major cultural values in embodied forms. By bowing, people send greetings, show respect, or thank other people, *kami,* and *hotoke.* Cleaning and purification maintain boundaries and order both in everyday life and on ritual occasions. Gratitude and a sense of indebtedness to others become concretized in the foods, drinks, greetings, and goods that others receive. Similarly, by making offerings and bowing to *kami* and *hotoke,* one thanks them for past favors or expresses gratitude for their protection in general. The values of purity and cleanliness, reciprocity and connectedness, and knowing indebtedness to others are not written in sacred texts, verbally articulated, or learned in religious institutions but become *embodied* during rituals. These key ritual actions, therefore, bring "saying" and "doing" together in the process of embodiment (cf. Giddens 1984).

The embodiment of moral values is by no means limited to ritual contexts. In everyday life, adults often comment on the posture of children when they are standing or sitting: stand up straight, keep your legs together, don't lean on one leg or the other. Properly acting bodies are morally valued bodies. Similarly, a Zen priest's talk on the day of the vernal equinox—a conventional time to visit family graves—highlighted the embodied nature of Japanese morality. After discussing the importance of ancestors and of transmitting the value of filial piety to the next generation, the Zen priest said: "What can we teach our children to make them good Japanese people? We should teach them to speak the Japanese language correctly. We should teach them to use chopsticks correctly. We should also teach them to place their shoes together when they take them off." In other words, these orderly actions are thought to produce good Japanese people—they provide culturally specific forms of moral discipline. These seemingly mundane, everyday practices—one cannot live one's life without speaking, eating, and returning to one's house—are much more than mere custom and manners; they contribute to a sense of moral order. Key ritual actions such as bowing, cleaning, and offering empower a moral order pervasive in everyday life: they embody what it means to be a good Japanese person. As such, key ritual actions possibly engage people in a deeply emotional manner.

Although key ritual actions for *kami* and ancestors both embody important Japanese values, differences do exist at the level of cultural representation. A visit to a Shinto shrine is likened to a formal visit to a superior's house: ringing the bell, greeting *kami* (bowing), offering a gift (donation), attracting *kami*'s attention (clapping hands), and asking for a favor or thanking them for past favors (bowing, putting hands together) while concentrating (closing eyes).[7] A Shinto ritual is sometimes compared to receiving a special guest: cleaning and beautification (purification of ritual space), greeting the guest (bowing), preparing and presenting food and drink (offering), communicating with the guest (addressing the *kami*), and entertaining the guest (dance and music). While *kami* are treated respectfully as guests, ancestors are treated as special family members with not only respect but affection—unlike *kami* they are in-group members. As opposed to a Shinto shrine, a family grave is regularly cleaned because it is considered to be like one's own house. Just as people take care of their senior family members, so ancestors receive a variety of personalized offerings, including their favorite foods. Although, like *kami,* ancestors are shown respect, thanked for their protection, or petitioned, unlike *kami* they are offered prayers for their peaceful rest. Similarly, people care about their ancestors' feelings; they clean, offer food and drink, and decorate the grave with flowers to make them comfortable. Ancestors are also kept from feeling lonely. Such considerations are less common for *kami*. Therefore, although ritual actions for *kami* and *hotoke* both embody common Japanese values, ritual acts for *kami* and ancestors remain differentiated: the ancestors are treated as cherished insiders and the *kami* as honored outsiders. This distinction corresponds to a fundamental contrast between the inside *(uchi)* and the outside *(soto)* in Japanese social life, a distinction repeatedly documented by Japan scholars (see, e.g., Kondo 1990 and Lebra 1996).

Actions Restricted to Ritual Contexts

Ritual life in Old Kamakura involves not only key actions but also the actions that highlight the discontinuity between ritual and mundane contexts. People explain the meanings of these restricting actions without referring to their use and meaning in everyday life. Clapping one's hands, offering evergreen branches, delivering the *norito* (ritual prayer) to *kami*—all are examples of restricting ritual actions.

Clapping Hands for *Kami,* Joining Hands for *Hotoke*

The Shinto manual cited earlier tells us that around the third century clapping was used to greet people of a high class (Jinja Honchō 1995, 90). People in Kamakura today use clapping in a similar way—to greet and show respect to *kami* at domestic altars and shrines. They also clap their hands to call the *kami*'s attention to their presence as well as their wishes, thanks, or the prayers they are about to make. In daily life, by contrast, clapping usually denotes praise after a performance or presentation. One interesting use of clapping in Kamakura is to indicate, or demarcate, time. One type of clapping *(sanbonjime)* is often employed to end a social gathering or banquet. The latter part of the term, *jime,* derives from the verb *"shimeru"* and means to bind, settle, tighten, or tie. The idea is that the clapping "settles," or concludes, a particular occasion. The organizer of the gathering often asks people to clap their hands ten times in a pattern consisting of three rapid triple claps and one final clap—an official time marker created communally at a social gathering. Clapping hands at a shrine, however, does not indicate a shift in time. Occasionally people may use clapping to attract others' attention when it is noisy—in a classroom, for example. I have even seen people clap their hands to attract the attention of carp in a pond. Such clapping, both in everyday life and at a shrine, attempts to attract attention. Unlike in regard to the act of bowing, however, people failed to explain the meaning of ritual clapping by referring to clapping in everyday life. Some simply reported that it is a matter of showing proper manners at a shrine; others said they just follow the instructions posted at the shrine.

Joining one's hands together for *hotoke* is considered an equivalent of clapping one's hands for *kami*.[8] Both acts signal the ritual encounter. Hands are joined together to petition, to pray, to thank, to show respect, to greet, to report, and to talk to *kami*, buddhas, or ancestors. Occasionally people in Japan join their hands together to beg for something in everyday life, but not to greet each other. Therefore, unlike the key actions that bridge ritual life and everyday life, clapping and joining one's hands are used to distinguish the ritual occasion.

Branches for *Kami*, Incense for *Hotoke*

Offering evergreen branches is another act confined mainly to ritual contexts. During a typical Shinto rite, the head priest as well as parishioners offer a piece of branch approximately 35 centimeters long. The ritual actor turns and directs the bottom part of the branch toward the altar as if handing it to *kami*. The Shinto manual cited earlier encourages people to offer a pair of branches at the altar twice a month, although not everybody follows this advice (Jinja Honchō 1995). The branches, the manual explains, are refreshing symbols of life (1995, 74). Informants were reluctant to offer religious or historical explanations regarding the branches, however; they often said they offer branches to *kami* simply because it is the custom. Like clapping one's hands, offering branches symbolizes a person's encounter with *kami*.

While offering evergreen branches is primarily reserved for *kami*, burning incense is an indispensable ritual act when facing *hotoke*. Incense is lit at the family altar and the family grave to beautify and purify with the scent. A few people told me that incense is considered a meal for *hotoke*. Although ancestors regularly receive cooked food that can be readily consumed by the living, incense would not be edible for the descendants. In this sense, burning incense as a meal for *hotoke* is an act that separates the dead from the living, thus setting the ritual offering apart from regular meals for mortals.

In daily life, people in Kamakura rarely burn incense for nonritual purposes; they associate incense primarily with venerating the dead. A small number of people, however, do learn the incense ceremony, whose origins are traced back to the Heian period. An incense ceremony teacher who lived a block away from my residence once told me that she distinguishes among scents just as she characterizes the tastes of food,—as sweet, bitter, sour, or tangy. Unlike in the tea ceremony, people rarely participate in the incense ceremony. I met no one who accounted for lighting incense for *hotoke* by referring to the incense ceremony.

Delivering the *Norito* and Chanting Sutras

Although most of the ritual actions for *kami* and *hotoke* consist of nonverbal acts conducted in silence, they also involve two main verbal acts: delivering the *norito* for *kami* and chanting sutras for *hotoke.* Ordinarily religious specialists perform these two acts.[9] The *norito,* recited by Shinto priests in formal, archaic Japanese, reverently asks *kami* to enjoy the offerings and protect the parishioners. Informants were often vague about the content of the *norito.* Some bluntly said it is unintelligible except for a few phrases and people's names. Yet they judged the performative quality of the delivery; some priests, they said, are more skilled and smoother than others.[10]

Just as delivering the *norito* symbolizes the ritual occasion for *kami,* so chanting sutras signals the occasion for buddhas and ancestors. Most informants emphasized the religious efficacy of chanting sutras—chanting is thought to ensure ancestors' peaceful rest. In the words of a female college student, sutras are "magic spells that make ancestors happy." Few laypersons explained the meaning of chanting sutras by referring to Buddhist doctrines or religious significance—to appreciate Buddha's teachings, for example, or learn lessons from sutras. Some informants simply told me that they do not know the reason for chanting sutras or do not understand their meaning. This is not surprising, though, for sutras are written in classical Chinese. Unlike the Bible, which has been translated into many languages, sutras are valued as performance. When I asked some questions about chanting on a ritual occasion, a young Zen priest told me, "If you are interested in the detailed meaning of the sutras we chanted today, you will have to talk to a professor studying them." At least, in his view, the primary job of a Zen priest is to chant sutras expertly as a ritual specialist, which takes primacy over studying the detailed meanings of individual sutras.[11]

Specialists and parishioners alike evaluate chanting as a performance with musical components. A Zen priest in his early forties told me that he enjoys chanting with older priests: "We get everything right. Bells come in at the right time, and we can coordinate our pitches." He complained about those who chant at their own pace and never try to adjust to others, which makes it a painful experience. Another priest in his late forties told me that he practices chanting every day and tries out different sutras—particularly those that are rarely chanted. People are also aware of the musical aspects of chanting. Nakagawa-*san*, a woman in her late fifties, proudly said, "The head monk of our family temple has a wonderful voice." My landlady—an enthusiastic opera fan—commented that a Buddhist ritual, involving instruments and human voices, is similar to a classical music performance. People also commented on whether chanting evokes feelings of gratitude. Some people complained that priests sometimes rush through the sutras. Others criticized young, inexperienced priests or those with hair. Proper appearance (shaven head) also has a positive influence on people's rating of a priest's chanting.

Embodiment and the Power of Ritual

Close examination of Japanese ritual acts, then, reveals the use of key actions and restricting actions that produce differentiation and resonance of meanings between the two realms of experience: ritual and daily life.[12] Key ritual actions are socially indispensable acts whose meaning echoes the everyday experiences of the participants. Ritual actors explain the significance of bowing during rituals—to thank, to show respect, or to ask a favor—in relation to the uses of bowing in daily life. And just as people give presents to thank, to ask a favor, and to send greetings in everyday life, so they make donations and offerings to *kami* and ancestors when asking a favor, thanking them for a past favor, or sending greetings. Furthermore, people value these key actions both aesthetically and politically. They have the power to negotiate social relations and identities.

Unlike the common assumption in the social sciences that religious activities imply the presence of a religious belief behind them (church attendance is often used as an indicator of religious belief), Ian Reader maintains that ritual "action precedes belief" in Japan. He continues: "Situations demand actions that express a latent religiosity. . . . [W]hen performed with purity and sincerity of mind, the traditional and socially prescribed reactions to the situation of death are not simply formalistic, but become vehicles of religious expression" (1991, 15–16). The key ritual actions discussed in this chapter embody a moral order that prevails in Japanese social life, which makes ritual—"the traditional and socially prescribed reactions"—a powerful vehicle indeed for deep emotional engagement. And hence, as informants often say, rituals evoke a good, fresh feeling.[13]

While key actions function as resonators of meaning between the world of ritual and everyday life, restricting actions set the ritual context apart. Because of their infrequent use in everyday life, clapping and joining hands, offering branches, delivering the *norito,* and chanting sutras are often taken as the essence of ritual actions for *kami* and *hotoke.* They symbolize encounters with *kami,* buddhas, and ancestors.

Instead of externalizing the moral order in a religious doctrine or sacred text, common ritual actions evoke moral meaning in an embodied form. The power of ritual in Kamakura resides in its ability to privilege the established moral order that pervades everyday life (cf. Bell 1992). Key ritual actions evoke the moral values maintained in everyday life; restricting ritual actions differentiate and highlight the very presentation of the embodied order in a privileged manner. Such resonance and separation occur in *bodily* terms rather than in the form of thought —that is, in cognitive terms (cf. J. Z. Smith 1987). The combination of these two categories of action makes ritual a complex orchestration of embodied meanings.[14]

CHAPTER 3

Emplacing Moral Order

Ritual and Everyday Environments

"What are you doing? Stop that right now, please!" A young trainee at a Shinto shrine raised his voice when he discovered a group of amateur photographers taking pictures of the head priest during a ritual. The trainee was dressed in white and light blue—ranks of Shinto priests are easily known by the colors of their dress. I had seen this young man many times on ritual occasions. Usually he stood calmly and politely outside the immediate ritual site. Why was he so upset today? As photographing the shrine and rituals occurs on a regular basis at this renowned shrine, this could not be the sole reason why the trainee was distressed. Indeed, the shrine receives many tourists and usually allows people to use their cameras. But photographing is seriously discouraged in areas that are "higher" and thus closer to the presence of *kami*. On this day photographers were taking snapshots from the wrong place. Standing at the side of the shrine compound, they were photographing the Shinto priest at the door of the *shinden:* the house of *kami.* These photographers could be compared to people looking into the house of a VIP through a side window that happens to be open and taking pictures of the festivities inside the house. Such an important person, or *kami,* should be visited from the main door, in a formal way, with appropriate greetings. And the *shinden,* where *kami* descend, must be protected from unapproved viewing and is located in the innermost area, with limited access. Thus the trainee was restoring right order in a ritual environment disturbed by these cameramen.

During a ritual, as this case illustrates, interacting bodies and environments generate a variety of cultural meanings: purity and impurity, respect and disrespect, formality and informality. In Chapter 2 we explored the ways in which ritual actions embody moral values and meaning—the act of cleaning, for example, embodies the morally positive value of purity. This chapter will examine moral meanings that become embodied in places. I refer to such a process—the embodiment of meaning and value in the environment—as *emplacement*. Based on the works of the philosopher Edward Casey (1996), I define emplacement as two processes: (1) collecting and guiding of objects and bodies according to culturally defined and socially generated environments; and (2), in so doing, creating and maintaining culturally defined and socially generated environments as they collect objects and bodies in a culturally specific way. In the case of Kamakura, ordering objects and bodies in certain ways has a moral significance.[1] The act of cleaning, for instance, creates or maintains a pure and morally positive environment, thereby *emplacing* the idea of purity.

The concept of emplacement is useful because it highlights qualitative, concrete, and subjectively anchored environments of which people are part and with which they interact. Among the Western Apache, for example, places "stalk" people with moral stories (Basso 1984). If the Western Apache were to lose their land onto which these moral stories are emplaced, they would suffer serious damage to their moral system. In this sense, just as places are part of people, people are part of places. Furthermore, as the Western Apache live their lives, places acquire new stories. Thus the environment not only constitutes an active force that guides people's actions, it also develops as people develop.

These ideas of emplacement present opportunities to reconsider cherished notions of self and space in Western thought. Contesting the images of the environment as a static, fixed, and passive background (Rodman 1992), the idea of emplacement emphasizes the process of the environment's "becoming" (cf. Strathern 1996, 203). Such a view of the environment stands in opposition to the notion of space prevalent in scientific discourses—as a quantifiable, abstract, and objectified environment external to human existence and independent of people's subjective experiences. Moreover, the emplacement of moral meanings and practices challenges the primacy of mind over body and subject over object in people's moral systems. The body and the environment are presumed to play an insignificant role in complex mental phenomena —such as moral systems.[2]

A focus on emplacement also resonates with two central themes in many Japanese rituals: community protection and defense of boundaries. The goal of community protection is commonly found in the analyses of Shinto rituals and community festivals in many parts of Japan (Bestor 1989; Nelson 2000; Robertson 1991; Schnell 1999). Purification and defense of boundaries, moreover, are major elements in Japanese folk religion (Martinez 1998, 213). In Kamakura, too, local festivals typically involve purification of the neighborhood and its residents. By carrying portable shrines containing a neighborhood's tutelary *kami,* its residents delineate its boundaries as they parade on all the major streets. Here the act of purifying and protecting the community is a way of separating morally pure places—such as neighborhoods and residents' houses—from the rest. Using the idea of emplacement, then, this chapter will explore the creation of ordered environments and their moral significance by highlighting the culturally defined, hierarchical structures of ritual bodies and environments, discovering parallels between the structures and meanings of ritual versus everyday environments, and seeing how these structures are actively re-created.

Orienting Bodies

In both ritual and everyday life, bodies consist of hierarchically organized upper and lower parts—for example, the head and feet. The highest part of the ritual body, the head, is used to produce hierarchy in ritual contexts. The upper *(ue, kami)* is linked with such concepts as respect, high rank, nobility, and cleanliness; the lower *(shita, shimo)* is linked with such notions as low rank, vulgarity, and dirt. Hierarchy, respect, and social distance are maintained by orienting the upper and lower parts of not only bodies but objects.[3]

Bowing on the lowly earth floor, for example, is a dramatic way of displaying unequal social relations. During the Edo period, such a bow was the proper bodily position for commoners greeting the processions of feudal lords. Although it is no longer a feature of the daily routine, one may bow on the floor to a person when one wishes to express a deep sense of gratitude, to extend an apology for a serious offense, or to beg desperately for something. When the Green Cross Company was accused of having intentionally supplied unsafe blood products, even after the Japanese government had received AIDS warnings from American medical authorities, company executives apologized to the group of plaintiffs, who had become HIV-positive due to transfusions from the company's tainted blood, with such a bow (*Yomiuri Newspaper* 1996b).

Lowering the highest portion of the body is used to show respect in ritual contexts as well. Ishii-*san,* one of the caretakers of a Zen temple, explained: "Your head is the highest portion of your body. So bowing means lowering yourself further down than the person you are facing." Buddhist priests in the Zen, Jōdo, and Nichiren traditions in Kamakura use formal bows on the ground while facing the main ceremonial altar. Usually they spread a cloth to create a barrier between themselves and the ground, thereby preventing their contact with dirt. The hierarchical relationship between priests and objects of ritual attention is produced by the vertical distance created between the head of the priest and the head of the principal image.[4] Similarly, during a Shinto rite, the priest purifies participants by waving a ritual wand—commonly a wooden rod with white paper decorations—over their heads. Thus the power of the *kami* residing in the wand of purification is cast over the highest body part of parishioners.

Just as the vertical hierarchy is invested with cultural meaning, so too is the horizontal hierarchy: the front *(omote)* is associated with formality, centrality, respect, purity, and masculinity; the back *(ura),* with informality, disrespect, impurity, and femininity. Both during rites and in daily life, a maximum effort is made to avoid turning the back toward others or ritual targets, because turning the back shows disrespect. People told me that it is particularly disrespectful to turn your back to "those you respect," "those who are older or superior," and "people related to you." Similarly, a fifty-seven-year-old self-employed man told me: "It is important to face *kami* and buddhas—just as you face your superior." Because it is respectful to sit down facing buddhas and *kami,* nearby areas are usually guarded carefully in ritual contexts. When a ceremony was held at a Zen temple, priests carefully guided onlookers to the seating areas surrounding the central ritual space (Figure 5). Some newcomers, paying attention only to the central ritual space, sat in the guarded space and turned their backs to the principal image. Priests came out each time and asked them to move, pointing out the principal image. Whenever a talk is given in this ceremonial hall, the speaker's podium is set up on the left side of the room in relation to the principal image; this way, neither speakers nor listeners turn their back on it.

When it is difficult to avoid turning one's back toward others or objects of ritual attention, multiple bows may be used. When guests leave, they bow to their host in the guest room, and often again at the entrance. And if the host is seeing them off, they may bow yet again at the gate. Similarly, when Shinto priests leave the altar during a ritual, they bow to the altar, turn their backs as they walk away, then turn around again and bow to the altar at a gate or some other boundary to the innermost ritual space. When I visited a Shinto shrine with Zen priests, they showed me another strategy: they stepped backwards away from the central gate and then sideways away from the area that is visible from the *kami*'s vantage point.

When people must turn their back toward others or targets of ritual attention, an apology is called for. At the monthly Buddhist ritual at a prayer temple, the head priest sits facing the main altar while the followers seated behind him are also facing the altar. Right before a ritual began, a woman in her sixties turned around and said to a man in his seventies seated behind her, "I am sorry that I always turn my back to you." During a Shinto ritual held at a kindergarten run by a shrine, a children's dance replaced a typical shrine maidens' dance to entertain *kami*. At this point teacher stood up and announced: "Let's apologize to the *kami* for turning your backs to them when you dance. You'll dance

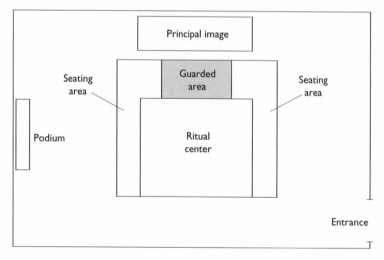

Figure 5. Floor Plan of a Ceremonial Hall in a Zen Temple

facing your parents today, but this is an exception." The children's dance was dedicated to *kami,* but the teachers wanted to show it to their parents too. The teachers solved this problem of having two targets of attention by telling the children to apologize to the *kami.*

Objects as well as bodies are carefully oriented in relation to other objects or persons in ritual and everyday life. Some objects have "head" and "tail" parts, "front" and "back," and these are oriented to the receiver accordingly. When handing a paper fan, one should hold the top part so the recipient can take the handle. When giving presents, the giver orients the gift so that the receiver can read the giver's name on the front wrapping paper. During tea ceremonies, the server hands a tea bowl with the decorated front side facing the guest. An instructor of Japanese language at an American university teaches her students how to exchange business cards; they should be turned so that the characters are oriented correctly for a recipient. The instructor said, "It takes a while for them to learn how." A student has to take out a card, turn it to face to the receiver, and hand it over while receiving that person's card in return. Even the simple act of exchanging business cards is conducted by bodies trained in a cultural milieu different from the one in which these students were socialized. Similarly, a person learns to offer evergreen branches to *kami* by considering the horizontal orientation of bodies and objects. Parishioners use the right hand to hold the branch and the left hand to support it. Then they turn the branch around to point the bottom toward the altar and put it down on the offering table —as if handing the branch to a *kami* seated across the table.

Using a House, Using a Ritual Place

Just as the body consists of qualitatively defined parts, so a place—a house, room, shrine, or temple—also consists of qualitatively distinct areas such as front and back or interior and exterior. People orient themselves with these characteristics of bodies and places in mind. When I was staying with the Dōmotos, for instance, the family and I returned to their house from a restaurant one evening and all the family members headed toward the back door. I followed them, but the head of the house told me: "Please, use the front gate. It takes many more years before you can use the back door." A close female friend of the Dōmotos used the back door just like the family members. As a formal guest, I was expected to enter the house through the large, elaborate front gate. The Dōmotos, a long-standing, landholding family of local fame, valued formality more than less wealthy and influential families in the community did. In their view, their guest—the outsider of high status—should use the front entrance. Meanwhile outsiders of low status, such as delivery people, customarily could not use the front door unless they were invited to do so.

It is a common practice for guests to use the front door in Kamakura as well as in other parts of Japan. Yet an anthropologist could be ushered in through the back door if he or she were considered more a neighbor or close acquaintance than a special guest. Furthermore, depending on class, occupation, region, personality, and the context of interaction, people might not be too concerned about or strategically contest formality. Nonetheless, bodies act in culturally defined places, and their actions generate a variety of cultural meanings: respect and disrespect, formality and informality, purity and impurity. The point here is not to generalize about whether or not an anthropologist is usually ushered in through the front door, but to emphasize that people construct culturally defined places in which they are embedded.

Using a House

The typical house in Kamakura has a front and a back entrance and is separated into a penetrable exterior and an inaccessible interior.[5] The front entrance is used by visitors of high social status or on formal occasions; the back entrance, in contrast, is associated with visitors of low social status (say, delivery people) and informal exchanges. The house of a renowned merchant family in Nagoya has a special front gate where feudal lords were once received. Similarly, a prestigious Zen temple in Kamakura has a special front gate originally used to receive imperial messengers. The gate is closed on ordinary days and is opened only for special ceremonies.

In Kamakura, the kitchen and the tearoom *(chanoma)* are located at the back of the house. In these rooms, the behavior and language are characterized by informality (Kondo 1990, 145). Whether one is allowed to enter the kitchen or tearoom is determined by social distance. A close family friend may help in the kitchen, but not an honored guest. As I got to know informants better, I was sometimes invited to spend time in their tearooms.

The formal guest room *(zashiki)* is usually located in the interior zone of a house, and people sit on flat, square cushions on the tatami-matted floor at a low table, with their legs folded.[6] The behavior and language used in the guest room are characterized by formality—formal sitting posture and the use of polite language (Kondo 1990, 144–145). The alcove indicates the upper end of the room, and the seat closest to the alcove is called the upper seat. Stepping into the alcove area is disrespectful—mixing the lower portion of the body with the upper portion of the room violates the order in a Japanese home. The area close to the doorway, on the other hand, is the lower end of the room, and the seat closest to the doorway is called the lower seat. The guest with the highest social rank and the most importance sits at the upper seat. The lower seat is reserved for those of a lower social rank. Although this arrangement sounds like a simple rule, things are more complex in real situations.

A merchant's house I visited had multiple guest rooms arranged in hierarchical zones, with the most elaborate room in the innermost part of the house.[7] I was first entertained in the exterior guest room, but during my second visit I was shown a special tearoom, used to receive feudal lords in the past, and the larger guest room located in the innermost zone reserved for prestigious guests such as members of the imperial family. Clearly I was not a guest of high rank to be entertained in these rooms.

In addition to the matters of social rank and distance, a Japanese house is gendered. The formal guest room is associated with males, while the kitchen and tearoom are linked with females. A woman from a white-collar family told me that her mother, a homemaker, started cleaning her kitchen extensively whenever she quarreled with her husband. This informant explained, "The kitchen was the only place my mother had for herself."

Japanese houses are differentiated vertically, too, by changing the floor levels slightly (Ueda 1974, 88). The raised floor is associated with formality and with people of higher social rank; the entrance floor connotes informality and people of lower social rank. On the first floor, the greatest difference in height exists between the entrance area and the corridor. Guests step up to the raised floor of the house for formal interactions. When entering the raised floor area, visitors must take off their shoes to differentiate the "pure" inside world from the "dirty" world outside. Although uninvited persons of lesser social status do not enter the interior zone of the house (the formal guest room, for example) and are confined to the "low" entrance-floor level, people of higher social status, when pressed for time, may hold casual conversations on the lower floor.

Noda-*san,* a kindergarten teacher in her fifties, told me that her husband's colleagues tease him about having such a "traditional" Japanese wife. When she greets them at the entrance, she sits formally on the raised floor and bows. A traditional Japanese house such as Noda-*san*'s is equipped with floors at different levels, sliding screens, and tatami rooms. If she were to stand on the raised floor and greet a guest standing on the entrance-level floor, her head would be higher than the guest's, which would be disrespectful. Noda-*san* confided: "For me, bowing on the floor is a matter of avoiding looking down upon guests at the traditional Japanese entrance. I am not particularly subservient." During my return trip to Kamakura in 2002, I noticed that a "barrier-free" home without vertical floor differences—thus accessible to a person in a wheelchair—is gaining popularity in Japan's aging society. It would be an interesting path for investigation to examine the ways in which people re-create or diminish emplaced hierarchies in "barrier-free" homes.

While the structure of the house may guide people's bodies, it does not *determine* these actions. A sweetmaker told me that the nouveaux riches in Kamakura tended to be arrogant and often instructed him to use the back door when delivering sweets. He said, "The long-standing upper-class families, on the other hand, did not care much about such things and sometimes invited me to use the front gate." The newly wealthy consciously differentiated merchants from guests by strictly imposing different entrances on them.

Using a Shrine

A Japanese shrine, just like a Japanese house, is organized by front/back, exterior/interior, and upper/lower distinctions. Like many shrines in Japan, the tutelary shrine in the community of Sakae consists of multiple zones leading from the exterior toward the interior area where *kami* descend. A shrine is structured as if it were wrapped in multiple layers that give it depth (Hendry 1993). A kind of rope made by twisting straw (*shimenawa*) hangs around the upper part of the torii gate.

According to the oldest anthology of poems in Japan *(Man'yōshū)*, a bound artifact indicated possession of the artifact itself or the occupation of land in ancient Japan (Nitscheke 1993, 95). The rope at a Shinto shrine signals *kami*'s possession of objects and occupation of places, such as the shrine compound. A pair of sculpted imaginary beasts resembling long-haired dogs guard the entrance to the shrine compound near the second torii gate. Torii gates, vertical gaps, statues, ropes—all these elements, in effect, wrap around the innermost area dedicated to *kami*.

The torii gate area—the exterior zone—is used for quick and casual greetings and is located farthest away from the shrine building. The exterior is exposed, accessible, and public. The gate represents the "front" of the shrine; therefore, people paying a formal visit to *kami* go through the front gate. The side gate connecting the shrine compound to the adjacent priest's residence, in contrast, is not used for these formal rituals but is reserved for informal visits. A few paces from the front gate, the visitor finds a narrow path—a prelude to encountering the *kami* located in the interior. The interior zone is protected, inaccessible, and private. The main shrine building accommodates the ceremonial hall. On ordinary days, a parishioner normally greets the *kami* at the hall's entrance—yet another boundary protecting the interior. The floor of the ceremonial hall is raised, and on special ritual occasions visitors must remove their shoes and take a few steps to the raised platform. Here the boundary is set by different floor levels. The altar to *kami* is located in the innermost portion of the shrine. The object upon which *kami* descend *(goshintai)* rests in the inner shrine, protected from the public gaze. Thus invisibility adds another barrier to secure the place for *kami*.

Similar vertical and horizontal hierarchies are found in temporary ritual places set up outside. During a winter festival in the neighborhood of Takane, four bamboo poles, tied with ropes, establish a square ritual place on the beach (Figure 6). Inside this ritual site the main altar stands closest to the sea—the higher and interior zone. The entrance is set up on the side away from the sea—lower and exterior zone. The seat closest to the altar, the "highest" seat, is reserved for the head priest. During the winter festival that I witnessed, however, a photographer and some little boys invaded the "higher" areas reserved for *kami*. After the rite had finished, an amateur cameraman in his sixties drew a picture of the ritual place to explain what had happened (Figure 7). He drew lines at forty-five-degree angles to the bounded square made by bamboo poles and then shaded the prohibited area behind the altar: "One should not enter this zone during the ritual." Usually the guards prevent onlookers from invading the prohibited zone, or sometimes the shrine is structured to protect the zone. Yet, in the case of this winter festival, the *kami* is in the sea, beyond the main altar. The cameraman said, "This should be obvious if you think about the purpose of this ritual—to pray for safety at sea and for the prosperity of the fishery." The prohibited zone stands between the *kami* and the people who are communicating with them. Thus, entering the shaded zone is like walking between a person of lower rank talking politely to a person of higher rank. The cameraman then drew my attention to the action of a Shinto priest who shot arrows into the four corners of the ritual site as he danced for the *kami*. Facing the altar, he set the fifth arrow in the bow but did not release it. This is because there is no evil beyond the altar, as it faces the *kami*. As for the photographer who entered the "high" area between the altar and the sea in order to get a good picture, my informant was unhappy. A photographer himself, he resented such behavior because it discourages the shrine from accepting cameramen at ritual sites.

Figure 6. The Winter Festival

Shaping the Place

As we have seen, in Kamakura, people actively order and maintain the environment in both ritual and daily life. They produce vertical and horizontal hierarchies by designing built environments, arranging objects, and placing persons. The owner of a Japanese tearoom in Kamakura, for example, told me that she designed her kitchen to be lower than the counter. "If I had the kitchen space at the same level as the seating area

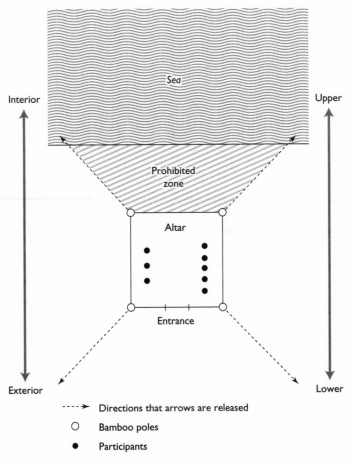

Figure 7. Diagram of the Ritual Site for the Winter Festival

for customers," she said, "I would be 'looking down' on the customers who are seated."

The vertical hierarchy also plays a role in shaping domestic and international relations in the political arena. When ritually affirming the appointment of a new prime minister, the Japanese emperor stands on a higher level than the premier, thereby expressing his higher rank. Ōi-san, a high school teacher in his fifties, told me that once there was a quarrel concerning the height of the podium—it was not clear by just how much "higher" the emperor outranked the prime minister. Ōi-san also told me that when Japan negotiated the first treaty at the end of the isolation period in the nineteenth century, there was a heated discussion over the physical arrangement of the meeting place: should the Japanese representatives sit in chairs or sit on the floor in the formal Japanese style? If they sat on the floor, they would be much lower than the foreigners seated in chairs. This meant that Japan would start the negotiation from an inferior position. Yet using chairs—an alien practice—was considered equally problematic. After long debate, representatives ended up sitting on chairs, but in the formal Japanese posture with legs folded. In this way they could use the Japanese-style posture and still maintain the same height—or social position—as the members of the foreign delegation. Seating arrangements constituted a significant part of the negotiation itself. Furthermore, during the Edo period, Japanese rulers maintained social hierarchy by differentiating the height of the floors where people stood. In fact, commoners could not freely build and use the raised floor (Ueda 1974, 88). In the Yonezawa domain in 1789, farmers were not allowed to have raised wooden floors because such pretensions were above their social rank. Although such laws no longer exist, the significance of producing and maintaining vertical hierarchy remains.

People construct a vertical hierarchy when setting up altars as well. In fact, they carefully choose pure and bright places as locations for houses, domestic altars, and family graves. People often prefer houses facing south, sited in a bright, sunny spot on a hillside, while they devalue a house that faces north and is set in a wet, shady spot. Similarly, the *kamidana* should be placed in a pure, bright place (Jinja Honchō 1995, 66). Meanwhile, a grave, like a house, is best sited in a sunny location on a hillside, not in a wet, shady spot. Interestingly, informants value purity and brightness not only as environmental qualities but also as aspects of people's personalities. Bright-hearted *(akarui)* persons are thought to have many friends; dark-hearted *(kurai)* persons are to be avoided. In elementary schools, students receive personality evaluations as well as grades for academic subjects. Teachers praise bright-hearted students and encourage all students to keep their bodies and belongings clean and pure. Thus positive personal qualities and positive environmental characteristics overlap.

A person maintains the purity of a ritual site by keeping a strict separation between "high" and "low." Since the upper portion of the house is associated with purity and the lower portion with dirt, the Shinto altar is typically sited in a high place near the ceiling. A Shinto manual discourages placing the altar where people on the floor above may walk over it—for example, in a multistory building or an apartment complex (Jinja Honchō 1995, 67). Placing anything above the altar, especially feet, the lower part of the body, disrupts the proper order and the ritual environment. When it is impossible to avoid setting up an altar on the first floor of a multistory building, the manual suggests two solutions (ibid.). First, a person can attach a piece of board to the ceiling right above the altar. Thus the board under the real ceiling creates a new "ceiling" for the altar, separating it from the world above and protecting the *kami* from being stepped on. Second, a person can place on the altar a piece of white paper with the character for "cloud" drawn on it in India ink. This creates a "sky with clouds" under the ceiling—an alternative to the real sky. Both the board and the piece of paper become tools for creating the "upper" zones when they are not available. Similarly, people protect the upper zone from contamination when they carry portable shrines under highway overpasses. All traffic, cars and pedestrians alike, is temporarily halted as the procession moves under the bridge.

Just as people protect the zone above *kami,* they also defend the area above the principal images at Buddhist temples. An electrician with many temple clients told me, "You're not supposed to lay electrical cords in the attic above the principal image." Moreover, the principal image at a Buddhist temple occupies a "high" place, symbolizing the highest mountain *(shumisen)* resting in the center of the world in the Buddhist cosmology. Similarly, there is a strong link between high places and the sacred; mountains are considered sacred homes for *kami* as well as the otherworld for souls of the dead (Grapard 1982, 199–200).

People position ritual objects in accord with the purity of a place. Paper talismans obtained at shrines and temples are commonly taped high up on a pillar or entrance to a home. One day, after attending a Shinto ritual, I went to a tearoom with a group of participants. Since the tea table was too narrow to accommodate Hata-*san*'s paper bag containing a talisman, she took the talisman out and placed it on the table: "It is disrespectful to place talismans on the floor."

In addition to vertical hierarchy, it is important to maintain strict horizontal hierarchy in social and ritual life. The seating order, for example, horizontally arranges bodies in an ordered setting with "head" and "tail." Multiple ranking systems—by gender, age, and power—come into play in determining the seating order in any situation. During formal meetings of the neighborhood federation in Tokyo, men tend to take the "interior" seats facing the street while women take "exterior" seats closer to the street. Theodore Bestor observes: "The most prestigious (and usually the oldest) men sit in the back corner, and the slightly younger men who hold the real reins of power in the neighborhood . . . sit just 'below' them" (1989, 191). Bestor reports that he himself usually sat on the men's side at the lower end of the room during his fieldwork. His wife took a seat close to the head of the women's tables. Yet during their farewell party they were the guests of honor and received upper seats. In addition to age, gender, and power, therefore, those who are the focus of attention are granted upper seats.

Indeed, my special status as guest played a role in securing an upper seat during a meeting for organizing a *bon* dance festival. (The festival is often held in a nonreligious setting today, but some, including this one in Kamakura, take place at Buddhist temples since the festival has a religious origin of consoling spirits of the dead.) The long table stretches from the upper end to the lower. The upper zone near the alcove accommodates Buddhist priests and older men; the lower-middle zone is used by younger men; the lower end of the table is occupied by women. Although I was the youngest person in the room, I received the next-best seat after the priest's. In this case my guest status trumped my age and gender.

To violate the seating order is to threaten the social and cultural order. When he was a graduate student, the sociologist Matthews Hamabata once took the highest seat by mistake during a party with upper-class Japanese and their guests. The guest of honor had been granted a small love seat while the host, the guest of honor's wife, and others were properly positioned below the sofa area. In all innocence, however, Hamabata approached the guest of honor and shared the love seat with him. The consequences were humiliating: "The politicians' wives were pushed into very crowded corners near the entrance of the room . . . and as I sat down, a look of resigned disbelief crossed everyone's face" (Hamabata 1990, 12–13). As a student, of course, he should have remained in the "lower" entrance area.

I once had a similar experience of taking an upper seat by mistake. During a party with upper-class women, I was busy greeting the people I knew, and by the time I realized it was time to be seated, all of the middle and lower seats had already been taken. I asked a few people to give me the lower seat, but they stubbornly refused. In this competition to be polite, I was too slow and ended up taking the leftover seat that nobody else had claimed—one of the best seats in front of the alcove. Because of my embarrassment, I had trouble appreciating the elaborate meal on this occasion.

Horizontal hierarchy not only governs the placement of people but also the siting of domestic altars. When the *kamidana* and the family altar are in the same room, they must face in the same direction or else be placed at right angles to one another. If they were to face each other in the same room, a person would have to turn his or her back to one of the altars when performing rituals at the other. Moreover, one should not place an altar where people come and go; such a place is an "exterior" and lower portion of the room. Altars should be placed in the "interior" of the room, away from the doorway.

The idea of centrality is another criterion for the location of altars. Shinto and Buddhist manuals alike advise that altars should be found in central places (Ichikawa 1990, 106; Jinja Honchō 1995). In Kamakura, one of the central locations for domestic altars is the formal guest room, the innermost room reserved for important guests and formal occasions.[8] People sometimes place family altars in the living room. I know a family that lives in a large, old-fashioned house with a formal room for ancestors. Yet they decided to move the family altar from the special ancestors' room to the guest room because the ancestors' room was not "central" enough—it was not used very often.

Moral Order

In both ritual and everyday contexts, as we have seen, people constantly manage their bodies in culturally constructed places with upper, lower, front, back, exterior, and interior zones. As people bow, sit on the floor, face or turn away from others, and take the "higher" or "lower" seats, interactions between bodies and places generate cultural meanings such as purity versus impurity, respect versus disrespect, formality versus informality, and social distance versus proximity. Furthermore, people actively order these places when they have a house built or choose the location for a domestic altar.

Pierre Bourdieu (1977, 94) usefully points out the moral implications of habitual bodily practices, such as standing up straight. Not always emphasized, however, are the moral possibilities of the environment. In Kamakura, sustaining an ordered universe contributes to maintaining a sense of what it means to be a good person.[9] When the order is violated, morally relevant questions arise concerning a person's reputation and upbringing. Thus the embodiment of moral order accompanies the process of emplacement. Properly trained bodies operating in properly ordered places are vested with moral value. Moral bodies and places mutually shape one another.[10] Embodiment and emplacement complement each other in ordering the moral universe in ritual and everyday life in Kamakura.

But, what sets ritual apart from everyday life in this order making? One of the strengths of ritual derives from its power to simultaneously differentiate and resonate with everyday experience (Chapter 2; cf. J. Z. Smith 1987). Similarly, ritual use of place both resonates with and is distinguished from the ways in which people use places in daily life. For example, people place both domestic altars and special guests in the "upper" zone of "interior" rooms—away from the doorway and the "exterior" areas—by considering qualitative distinctions within a house. Just as the formal front gate of a shrine is reserved for special ceremonial occasions, so the front door of a house is used to receive guests of honor. Conversely, people use the back entrances of both houses and shrines for casual interactions. In both a ceremonial hall and a house, hierarchy is maintained by differentiating floor heights. Despite these parallels between the emplaced order in ritual and everyday contexts, ritual sites do carry symbols that distinguish them from mundane places.

Domestic altars accommodate special ritual utensils and offerings. The family altar usually contains the image of Buddha, ancestral tablets, an incense holder, an incense bowl, a ceremonial chime, and sometimes a variety of important documents and seals indicating the symbolic center of the house. The *kamidana,* sited high up near the ceiling, often contains amulets, evergreen branches, and offerings of raw food such as grains of rice and salt. Ritual's power, then, derives from its ability to differentiate and resonate with people's bodily and sited experiences in everyday life. Ritual produces not only privileged bodies (Bell 1992, 90) but also privileged environments—bodies and environments that are "higher" than their mundane counterparts. Above all, rituals empower the ordered nature of bodies and places pervasive in everyday life (cf. Ashkenazi 1993; Kalland 1995; McVeigh 1997; Reader 1991; Reader and Tanabe 1998; Schnell 1999; Smyers 1999). Such an integrated order is much more comprehensive than a religious order limited to a specific religious institution or doctrine.

Morality and Sociocentric Ideas of the Environment

The moral dimension of orderliness found in acting bodies and places sheds light on certain aspects of ritual life in Japan that some find puzzling. Japanese people often claim that they are not "religious" but still perform a series of ritual greetings to *kami* and buddhas at shrines and temples (Reader 1991, 1–4). If they are not religious, why do they engage in these greetings? The following case of Suzuki-*san* offers an illuminating example. Suzuki-*san,* a thirty-eight-year-old man who works for a major pharmaceutical company in Tokyo, converted to Christianity when he was in college. He maintains no domestic altars at home, nor does he go to shrines or temples for religious reasons. But when I asked him if he had ever sent ritual greetings to *kami* and buddhas since his conversion to Christianity, he replied: "Whenever I go back to my hometown in Shizuoka where I grew up, things are different. When I enter my natal home, I naturally greet *kami* and ancestors enshrined at domestic altars. When I face the bodhisattva Jizō, the protector of children, I recall my childhood and send a ritual greeting. There's something special about my natal home." Suzuki-*san* vividly demonstrates how the power of place—in this case the place where he was raised—has shaped his ritual action toward *kami,* ancestors, and the bodhisattva Jizō. When he returns to his hometown, this power guides his body along the path set long ago in his childhood—regardless of his later conversion to Christianity. Despite Suzuki-*san*'s assertion that he does not believe in *kami* or Buddhism, he reports that his natal home makes him feel "natural" about proffering his ritual greetings. This feeling comes from his knowledge of his natal home—the environment in which his body became enculturated. Considering that ritual empowers a sense of "what feels good and right" in everyday life, Suzuki-san's ritual act in his natal environment is not so much an expression of his personal faith in *kami* and buddhas as a sign of a good Japanese person following the inherent order.

Does this mean that Suzuki-*san* is not a serious believer in Christianity? Is he "religious" only in certain places? Does his sense of morality depend on where he is? The idea of contextual religiosity often carries an assumption that one's religious status is measured by one's exclusive commitment to a single religious tradition that consistently manifests itself in ritual activity. "Contextual morality" is also a problematic concept that would implicitly dismiss Suzuki-*san*'s behavior as inferior and deviant. Furthermore, the idea of contextual morality assumes an autonomous individual cut off from others as well from as the environment. In this view, the individual should be the independent locus of decision making and ultimately responsible for his or her own choices and actions. In these terms, morality is essentially contained within the entity of the individual. If answers to moral questions happen to vary according to context, the person is considered morally weak and thus inferior to those who uphold consistent standards regardless of the situation. But not all cultures worship the idea of the autonomous individual, and if the qualities of the perfect person vary from culture to culture, ideals of moral worth are also likely to differ. In fact, anthropologists have found that many non-Western cultures value a sociocentric notion of the person—a person found in the company of others (Shweder and Bourne 1991). A good Japanese person, for example, is defined by the relations he or she maintains with others (Kondo 1990). In so doing, this person also defines others in turn. The content of moral acts may change according to the relationships one maintains with others, because a person may have different duties and obligations toward different groups of people. As opposed to the idea of the autonomous individual, moral ideas in this context may appear to be found outside the person—in social relationships. This is not always the case, however, for individuals also *constitute* social relationships.

Not only are people connected in social relationships, but the merging of people and environment is not uncommon in many non-Western cultures studied by anthropologists. Leroy Little Bear, for example, a member of the Small Robe band of the Blood Indian Tribe of the Blackfoot Confederacy, questions the dichotomy between person and place:

> When our people say, "I am the environment, for the land and me are the same," a lot of non-Indians interpret those statements metaphorically. Why? Because in non-Indian society, everything is metaphorical. . . . Whenever you make a statement in English, A is B, that's a metaphor. . . . A good example of that is a simple statement like "It is raining." In most Indian languages, we just say, "Raining." It is not equal to something else. Rain is rain is rain. (Leroy Little Bear 1998, 15–16)

If the environment is not considered a category separate from the individual, then moral ideas and systems may well be manifest in the environment. Among the Western Apache, moral stories are attached to the landscape and evolve as people develop (Basso 1996). In Kamakura, the orderliness of the environment possesses a moral significance: a clean house embodies a morally positive state. Again, these moral ideas appear to be located outside the individual—in the environment—only if we assume that the individual is cut off from the environment. Yet this is not necessarily the case if people are thought to constitute the environment.

In this context, rather than using concepts such as personification or anthropomorphism, we need to explore sociocentric views of the environment. Suzuki-*san*'s narrative raises a theoretically interesting point: he recognizes the power of place—his natal place that has actively shaped his ritual actions such as greeting *kami*, ancestors, and the bodhisattva Jizō. Rather than regarding the body as active agent/subject and the place as passive environment/object, Suzuki-*san*'s narrative hints at the agency of the environment.[11]

Although the primacy of mind over body has frequently been challenged in anthropological writings (Lock and Scheper-Hughes 1987; Strathern 1996), the supremacy of the body over the environment has not. No longer is the body assumed to be a product of nature and biology. According to the idea of the mindful body (Lock and Scheper-Hughes 1987), the body has thoughts and ideas embodied in it. Nonetheless, place often remains a passive object that is mastered or at least internalized by the body as a full agent. Suzuki-*san*'s narrative contests such a view; Suzuki-*san*'s body is not necessarily the master of a passive environment (cf. Bourdieu 1977). A focus on sociocentric ideas of the environment, therefore, would be an interesting path to pursue, which allows us to reconsider people's moral embeddedness in their environments in cross-cultural contexts. And the recognition of such moral embeddedness would explain why the trainee described in the opening paragraph of this chapter was so upset when scolding the intrusive photographers. What they had violated was much more than socially prescribed manners: it was the cherished moral order emplaced in a ritual context.

CHAPTER 4

Constructing Kamakura In Everyday Life and City Festivals

Kamakura (39.53 square kilometers) is a city located in Kanagawa Prefecture in the Kantō region of Japan. It consists of five administrative districts: Kamakura (14.22 square kilometers), Koshigoe (4.21 square kilometers), Fukasawa (8.22 square kilometers), Ōfuna (8.40 square kilometers), and Tamanawa (4.48 square kilometers). Kamakura is approximately 50 kilometers away from Tokyo Station by the Yokosuka rail line. But simply reciting the city's spatial characteristics alone cannot convey the localized meanings emplaced in Kamakura. Many anthropological writings assume the "primacy of space over place" (Casey 1996); space is homogeneous, exchangeable, and quantifiable; places are considered simple coordinates in space. Yet it is essential to know the characteristics of Kamakura as a place if we are to understand the localized meanings and values that ritual actors create during city festivals.

Kamakura as a Place

Kamakura consists of numerous neighborhoods, the basic cultural unit that constitutes a city in Japan. Furthermore, neighborhoods and places in Old Kamakura—Hachimangū Shrine, the main street, the neighborhood of Sakae, the beach areas—are ordered in relation to each other. Similarly to ritual places, houses, and rooms (see Chapter 3), Kamakura and its neighborhoods are defined according to upper/lower, front/back, and exterior/interior distinctions. Upper, front, and interior connote formality, higher social class, and social distance; lower, back, and exterior are associated with informality, lower social class, and close social relations. It was during my apartment hunting that I first noted these distinctions ordering communities in Kamakura. When I was looking for a place to stay at the beginning of my fieldwork, I talked to Maeda-*san*, a middle-aged restaurant owner in her late forties, about the apartment in Kamakura I was thinking of renting. To my surprise, she rigorously discouraged me from doing so, because it is located in the "lower" part of the city. Since "lower" areas are less prestigious, Maeda-*san* insisted that I take an apartment in the "upper" part of town. Originally, I was introduced to Maeda-*san* by Yasuda-*san,* who is from an aristocratic family and a regular client at Maeda-*san*'s locally famous restaurant. Considering her association with upper-class clientele, Yasuda-*san*'s introduction, and my experience of studying abroad (a practice common among children from well-to-do families), Maeda-*san* tried to place me in a community "higher" than the one that I was considering.

Because people use various areas of Old Kamakura to create localized meaning in ritual contexts, one has to examine the immediate ritual environments—a shrine, a street, a beach—as they are situated in relation to each other in Old Kamakura. During citywide festivals, in which residents commonly participate, Old Kamakura itself becomes a large ritual place consisting of a constellation of ritual sites. To examine the meaning and strategy used in these city festivals, this chapter will first explore Kamakura as a subjectively experienced locality—a lived place. Kamakura's past as both capital and resort gives its residents two major discourses for constructing it. The city's past becomes further emplaced according to location hierarchies such as upper/lower, and front/back distinctions.

Two Historical Discourses: Kamakura as Capital and Resort

The structuring of Kamakura cannot be understood without considering two very different historical periods: as an ancient capital during the Kamakura period (1185–1333) and as a prestigious resort in the early twentieth century.[1] In the eyes of its residents, Kamakura's past as capital and resort represents the source of their pride in its uniqueness.

Minamoto no Yoritomo established the political organization of warriors, the Kamakura shogunate, in Old Kamakura—a narrow opening surrounded by mountains to the east, north, and west, and by Sagami Bay to the south. The shogunate initiated construction projects to convert seven narrow openings into mountain paths to facilitate transportation (Kamakura Shishi Hensan Iinkai 1990b, 60). Kamakura's city plan adopted features from Kyoto, the former capital of Japan. To parallel Kyoto's imperial palace, which occupies that city's "high" place, the tutelary shrine of the Minamoto clan (Hachimangū) was built. The shogun's residence was situated on the eastern side of the shrine so that the *kami* occupied a place "higher" than the shogunate (ibid., 1990b, 68). Meanwhile, the southeastern part of the town, "lower" than the northern area, bustled with merchants. The main street of Wakamiya Ōji took the place of Kyoto's Suzaku Ōji (ibid., 1990b, 66) and connected Hachimangū, located in the interior, to the exterior zone of Old Kamakura. During the Kamakura period, the main street was a restricted space; whoever entered this thoroughfare from side roads had to dismount and walk to the shrine in order to show respect. In 1182, Yoritomo is said to have built the raised stone pathway *(dankazura)* on the main street as a petition to the *kami* of Hachimangū that his wife, Masako, would safely deliver a child. Two major streets, Ima Ōji and Komachi Ōji, were built on both sides of the main street for everyday use.

Yoritomo's devotion to Hachimangū is also visible in his dedication of *yabusame* performances and sumo wrestling at the shrine. *Yabusame* ritualizes common training practices for warriors during the Kamakura period, when they fought on horseback using swords and bows and arrows. Warriors polished their skills during hunting and training sessions. The construction of Hachimangū and the dedication of ritual performances at the shrine were strategies to build a symbolic center for the warrior class in the new political regime. In the previous Heian period (794–1185), aristocrats had performed political rites centered on the emperor and the court. During the Kamakura period, however, rituals of appointing shoguns as well as calendrical rites of the shogunate were performed at Hachimangū, which came to protect not only the Minamoto clan but also the shogunate itself. In addition to Hachimangū, many well-known religious structures characterizing present-day Kamakura were built during the Kamakura period. Among them were the renowned Kenchōji and Engakuji temples of Rinzai Zen Buddhism and a landmark of Kamakura, the Great Buddha. The bronze statue, approximately 12 meters high and weighing 121 tons, survived a major earthquake of 1923.

Kamakura as a splendid resort in the early twentieth century is another image frequently evoked in both ritual and everyday life. In 1868, the long-standing Tokugawa shogunate ended, and the building of a new modern state began with the imperial restoration. In contrast to the Tokugawa shogunate's isolationist policy, which lasted for three hundred years, Japan reopened its doors to the world. Intellectuals encountered and adopted a range of Western ideas and practices in law, medicine, science, technology, and social customs. Among them were Western clothing, food, dance parties, and health resorts. Before the onset of the Meiji period (1868–1912), Kamakura had regressed to a collection of villages of minor importance, occasionally receiving pilgrims at its religious sites. But then the town was rediscovered by those in power and underwent dramatic transformations—this time, as a resort.

The Iwakura Delegation, sent to visit the United States and Europe between 1871 and 1873, was the first to see Kamakura's potential as a health resort (Shimamoto 1993, 15, 19–21). In 1872, the delegation visited Brighton, England, known as a seaside resort since the eighteenth century, and soon its members were buying second homes in Kamakura and vicinity. The delegation included famous politicians such as Iwakura Tomomi and Itō Hirobumi, the former lord of Maeda domain, Maeda Toshitsugu, and a doctor, Nagayo Sensai, who opened the first seaside sanatorium in Kamakura in 1887. Because of its pleasant climate and environment, Kamakura became a health resort for wealthy patients—particularly those with tuberculosis.

The first batch of summerhouses appeared in Kamakura in the 1890s. It was then that two railways—the Tōkaido Line and the Yokosuka Line—introduced service through the Kamakura area, which enabled people to reach Kamakura within two and a half hours from Shinbashi Station in Tokyo. By 1912, some 31 percent of Kamakura's population was composed of vacationers (Shimamoto 1993, 60–61). Because the number of wealthy nonresidents increased so rapidly, Kamakura's law of 1911 applied lower tax rates to inland areas and higher tax rates to the beach areas where many summer vacationers resided (Kamakura Shishi Hensan Iinkai 1990a, iii). The prestigious Japanese inn Mitsuhashi Ryokan, described in the novel *Naomi* by Tanizaki Junichirō (1985), stood in the beach area. In contrast to the higher status accorded the northern Hachimangū area during the

Middle Ages, the communities along the beach gained prestige during the resort era. Though the northern shrine areas did not lose their importance, the resort era introduced a new hierarchical order and the waterfront became the symbolic center of Kamakura for the nation's new elite.

Before the arrival of summer vacationers, Kamakura had consisted mainly of farming and fishing communities during the Edo period (1603–1868), except for a few artisans and merchants whose services were required by the religious establishments. As the town developed as a resort, however, demand for summerhouses brought prosperity to carpenters, artisans, and merchants. In 1914, the town of Kamakura had 1,725 households (11,336 people), and among them 481 were classified as second homes and 200 as businesses (Kamakura-Chō Yakuba 1914). New businesses grew quickly: stores selling lunch boxes for vacationers at the train station; the first production of Western-style ham to meet the tastes of the upper class; and the production of carved lacquerware for souvenirs. Hotels, inns, and rental summerhouses came to flourish. Merchants visited summerhouses every day to take orders and developed personal ties with clients. A Japanese sweetmaker, Tanaka-*san*, told me: "In my father's time, female customers used to call him to discuss problems in their lives. These days, however, people go to discount stores for good prices and convenience. When my father was alive, this was unthinkable."

The arrival of summer vacationers brought not only prosperity but friction to the community of Kamakura. Committed vacationers formed the Kamakura Club (Kamakura Dōjin Kai) to influence the politics of the town, "split between the snobbish summer vacationers and those townspeople making good money out of them" (Kamakura Dōjin Kai 1995, 16). The initiators of the club were the elite upper class: a count, a medical doctor, a former governor, a former banker, a town administrator, a lieutenant general, a professor, a former envoy extraordinary and minister plenipotentiary, a school principal, and a vice-admiral (ibid., 1995, 16–17). The purpose of the club was to "preserve historical sites and treasures; improve sanitary conditions; promote education; improve residents' manners and customs; foster industrial development; and promote other activities benefiting the public" (ibid., 1995, 18). Starting with twenty-three members, the club gradually grew to two hundred members by 1922, including natives of Kamakura. By promoting the welfare of Kamakura as a whole, the club came to bridge two different social groups to a degree: summer vacationers and native residents.

As Kamakura developed further, the number of middle-class, year-round residents increased, and they began to promote their interests as full-fledged residents. Dissatisfied because natives still called them "vacationers" and charged them steeper prices, they established the Shōnan Club in 1924 and began to purchase their daily supplies in bulk (Kamakura Shishi Hensan Iinkai 1990a, 434–435). These residents believed that they deserved fairer treatment than what tourists and temporary vacationers had to endure. Along with the Great Kantō Earthquake (1923) that suddenly interrupted Kamakura's prosperity as a resort, the establishment of the Shōnan Club symbolizes the transition of Kamakura from a resort to a residential city (Shimamoto 1993).

Ordering Old Kamakura

The basic city plan of the Kamakura period survives today (Figure 8), and contemporary residents of Kamakura make conscious efforts to preserve it. Municipal law protects the mountains surrounding Old Kamakura to the north, east, and west. Old Kamakura still has seven incoming roads, too, although now they are paved with asphalt and improved by modern tunnels. The present-day *dankazura* pathway lies 180 centimeters above the original one built by Yoritomo. Wakamiya Ōji remains the widest thoroughfare that gives residents a sense of orientation—it defines Old Kamakura as the compound of Hachimangū. Today, Hachimangū, housing the tutelary *kami* of Kamakura's residents, remains the symbolic center. Meanwhile, vacation homes in the beach-front neighborhoods have disappeared and smaller residential homes and corporate recuperation facilities have emerged. Nonetheless, these neighborhoods continue to derive their prestige from having been the center of the former resort area. Small-scale merchants continue to deliver daily necessities to their customers' homes. Kamakura's past as a former capital and resort shapes a sense of place for its residents.

Yet the historical discourses of Kamakura as capital and resort are not mapped directly onto a blank space but combine with hierarchical orders such as upper/lower, front/back, and exterior/interior distinctions. Upper/lower distinctions in Old Kamakura became evident when Maeda-*san* told me that the apartment I was interested in renting is located in Shitamachi (Low Town), an area "lower" than Yamanote (Hillside). Although Shitamachi and Yamanote are regionally specific distinctions that originated in Tokyo, I heard them used in Kamakura.[2] While Yamanote culture is preeminent in mainstream Japanese society, Kondo (1990, 57) observes that Shitamachi culture has its own way of placing itself as the home for a "more 'traditionally Japanese' ethos." Yamanote people are said to value privacy and exhibit "taste" in their language, manners, and lifestyle, while Shitamachi people are said to be "informal, warmhearted, emotional, quick to anger, and quick to forgive" (Kondo 1990, 63). Maeda-*san* prides herself on attracting upperclass clients to her restaurant; she dismissed Shitamachi and recommended that I take an apartment located in a former resort community.[3]

In a later phase of fieldwork I discovered that liminality (Turner 1966) characterizes the area accommodating the apartment I thought

Figure 8. Map of Kamakura City

about renting. In the area, there used to be a tunnel associated with ghosts and a crematorium. The tunnel is located "between" two places: Kamakura and another community; this area is located at the margins of Kamakura. Not only margins of the body, but also margins of a place (gates of a house, village boundaries, the seashore) become targets of ritual attention in Japan (cf. Douglas 1966, 126).[4] Japanese ethnologists have documented many rituals to dispell evil spirits performed at the waterfront as well, to protect a village's territory from illness and misfortune (e.g., see Miyata 1993, 40–41). Furthermore, the crematorium is the place that regularly receives the newly dead; it is the place for those who stand "between" the living and the full-fledged ancestors. Japanese people perform elaborate ancestral rites to gradually transform the dangerous newly dead into benevolent ancestors during a ritual cycle of thirty-three or fifty years. Thus it is no coincidence that ghosts appear in the area associated with the tunnel and the crematorium, and moreover, that the neighborhood associated with them is denigrated.

The front/back and exterior/interior distinctions also order Kamakura's communities. The front/back and exterior/interior zones of Kamakura's neighborhoods roughly correspond to the native/newcomer distinctions among residents (cf. Robertson 1991). A retired journalist said, "In Kamakura, those who live facing the old main streets tend to be natives who can trace their ancestry in Kamakura back for generations." Kamakura's development as a summer resort had a major impact on the rise of occupational and class distinctions between front/back streets and exterior/interior zones of a neighborhood. A map of Kamakura printed in 1799 shows a row of houses concentrated along the intersection of main streets but no houses in the interior zones (Sawa 1976, 26). During the early twentieth century, incoming upper-class families built or rented summerhouses on back streets and in interior portions of a neighborhood. Later, during the rapid urbanization that began in the 1960s, the neighborhood's interior portion became the residential zone for middle- and upper-middle-class families.[5]

In Sakae, where I lived during my fieldwork, architecturally the houses in the exterior and interior zones of the neighborhood embody contrasting social values and lifestyles. The merchants and artisans lead lives directed toward exteriorization. Often they are involved in the community's close-knit social network. Their houses, often facing the main street, are exposed to busy traffic. Many shops have large sliding glass doors, and some stores have shelves outside displaying merchandise. During business hours, these shops open up to the main street and transform it into an accessible and interactive area—the essence of a Japanese shopping street *(shōtengai).* Residents in the interior zone, by contrast, tend to be middle- and upper-middle-class professionals or employees of large corporations. Because they often commute to their workplaces outside Kamakura, they have a more modest social presence in the neighborhood. Walking down one of the neighborhood's narrow back streets, one finds many foreign cars—a sign of wealth seldom found in the exterior zone. Architecturally, hedges, formal gates, and fences of stone and bamboo shelter the houses in the interior. Residents in the interior thus share certain similarities with the former nobility (Lebra 1996), who positioned themselves at the ceremonial "front" in public scenes yet remained in relative seclusion in their private lives. These residents, too, have a tendency toward interiorization in their private lives while simultaneously being at the "front" as the driving force in mainstream Japanese society.

The tension between residents in the exterior and interior zones of Sakae is manifest in daily life. The head of Sakae's business association complained, "People in the interior do not always listen to us [in the exterior]." When he suggested that they should have the back streets widened for the fire truck, the people in the interior rejected the idea because doing so would invite unwanted cars, even though private cars were uncommon at the time. The head of the business association continued, "Now that everybody has a car, people in the interior complain that their streets are too narrow to park their cars." The tension between the exterior and interior zones becomes especially sharp during the annual festival of the neighborhood shrine (see Chapter 5). When the ritual procession parades through all the major streets in Sakae, residents are supposed to come out to the street and greet it. Yet an informant told me, "These people in the interior do not come out very much." Businesspeople also complained that those living in the interior frequently fail to make festival donations or send portable shrine bearers.

In discussing the city's former mayors, a forty-three-year-old man neatly summarized the tension that divides Kamakura's residents: "Kamakura has had and currently has two strata, the natives and the incoming cultured people." He told me that mayors come from these two backgrounds in alternation and, interestingly, never last for more than one term of their appointment. And these two groups compete to construct Kamakura in their daily and ritual lives.

Constructing Everyday Kamakura

People in Kamakura use the city's past selectively—as a former capital and a resort—to construct Kamakura as a place. Kamakura is often represented as a historic capital *(shito),* or an old capital *(koto),* in municipal documents, advertisements, guidebooks, and articles in newspapers and popular magazines. The other self-representation is the image of a city rich in natural resources, including the bay and the mountains. Although these two images of Kamakura were already emerging during the city's resort days, it was not until the postwar years that they became firmly established. An early article in *Asahi Newspaper* dated 30 August 1933, for example, discussed urban development plans in Kamakura. It reported that "an urban planning proposal was presented at the committee to protect the town of Kamakura as an area of greenery. This would eternally preserve the historic city of Kamakura" (Kamakura Shishi Hensan Iinkai 1990a, 497). When Kamakura declared itself a city of peace in 1958, it was described as "possessing numerous historic ruins and a cultural heritage" (ibid., 1990a, 620). When the Association for Environmental Preservation (Fūchi Hozon Kai) was formed in 1964, it declared: "Kamakura is blessed with a striking natural environment and rich cultural resources" (Kamakura Shishi Hensan Iinkai 1990a, 620). Similarly, the charter of Kamakura Citizens of 1973 proclaims: "Kamakura is an ancient capital that is blessed with the beautiful natural resources of the sea and the mountains and a rich historical heritage" (ibid.,1990a, 628).

Kamakura's past history as an ancient capital is not confined to the images employed by the media and in municipal documents, however, but penetrates residents' everyday experience. In all parts of Old Kamakura, children find archaeological remains from the Kamakura period when playing outside, while adults find them when houses and buildings are being constructed. The city mandates that residents must pay for the excavation of archaeological artifacts found during construction on their property, which could cost an extra $100,000 for excavation and related expenses. When the city started a construction project for a long-awaited underground parking garage near the beach, numerous bones dating from the Kamakura period were found and the project was seriously delayed by archaeological surveys.

I myself experienced the sense of place that reigns in Kamakura when I had a chance to explore a medieval cave behind my landlady's house. Facing a clear stream, her house is surrounded by many large trees. In summer, cicadas sing noisily, squirrels play, and snakes, mosquitoes, and centipedes flourish. The cave is located in a long and narrow slit (*yato*), a ravine, spread out along the hillside. The cave is said to have belonged to the Hiki clan during the Kamakura period. One clan member became a nursemaid for the second shogun Yoriie, while another one became a secondary wife of Yoriie and bore him a son—a potential heir of the shogun.[6] But the Hōjō family, political rivals, wiped out the Hiki family, including the son of the shogun, in 1203. Some Hiki people were said to have escaped the assault and come to the cave. During World War II, a former resident had a shelter built on the hillside, and his construction crew discovered the bones of samurai warriors in the cave—positioned in the formal posture with their swords in their hands, indicating that they had committed ritual suicide. The owner of the house had the skeletons moved to a museum and requested a purification ritual. Mysteriously, after finding the skeletons, his family began to decline. Eventually they moved to Tokyo, but even after the former owner's family moved out, the previous owner's wife sometimes came back to the cave to pour rice wine for purification and to pacify the warriors' spirits. My landlady commented, "She seemed to connect their disturbance of the site of the ritual suicide with her family's decline."

On a clear autumn afternoon my landlady showed my husband and me around the cave. It consisted of six or more large rooms that probably could have held more than a hundred people. Small shelves were carved into the wall, perhaps to hold lights. Along the wall there were ditches. In the cave, my husband found four small pieces of delicate bone that he claimed might be finger bones of the medieval warriors. When I called an archaeologist, the son of an informant, he made me worried: "If they are human bones less than a hundred years old, you will have to report your finding to the local police for investigation. If not, however, register them as archaeological artifacts at the city office." Since the cave was on my landlady's land, our finding the bones might mean that the landowner would have to pay for the costs of excavation. Two weeks later, I had the archaeologist examine the bones. Upon opening the package, he immediately declared, "Twentieth-century raccoon bones!" Although our search for ancient warriors' remains was unsuccessful, this story does illustrate the sense of place that reigns in Kamakura. After all, their current city lies just above the ancient capital.

In daily life, people also evoke images of the ancient capital by connecting their place of residence to certain historical incidents and figures. Although there are no walls or monuments demarcating its boundaries, residents say the "real" Kamakura is not the administrative unit of Kamakura City but Old Kamakura, where the ancient capital used to stand. Speaking of a place in Kamakura City but outside Old Kamakura, people will say "Such-and-such is not really Kamakura." Few people questioned the imputed superiority of Old Kamakura over New Kamakura.

Regardless of descent, businesspeople exploit the image of Kamakura as a former capital to their advantage. Dove-shaped cookies—one of the city's most famous souvenirs—were first produced during the 1890s. The dove is strategically used as the logo because it is considered the messenger of the *kami* venerated at Hachimangū. Similarly, modern-day sword shops evoke the image of Kamakura as a capital for medieval warriors. In Sakae, although contemporary merchants and artisans are not direct descendants of their counterparts in the Middle Ages, they proudly announce that the Kamakura shogunate made Sakae an official business district. Furthermore, singing is used during gatherings and banquets to evoke images of the Kamakura period.[7] As a volunteer member of Sakae's welfare bureau, I participated in many banquets with the district's welfare commissioners. On several occasions, the head of the Sakae welfare bureau requested a song describing a train arriving in Kamakura and the large ginkgo tree at Hachimangū, where the third shogun of Kamakura shogunate was assassinated by his nephew. After singing this piece, the head of the welfare bureau proudly said: "Now, everybody, aren't we happy that we live in this famous old city, Kamakura? And we live in the oldest part of Old Kamakura— Sakae!"

Preservation Laws and the Ethos of Residents

Awareness that Kamakura is a city with a rich cultural heritage and a beautiful natural environment has fostered citizens' movements against development. An opposition movement led to the adoption of a measure known as the Special Municipal Law concerning the Preservation of Ancient Capitals (Koto Hozon Hō) in 1966. Established in the context of rapid economic growth between the late 1950s and the early 1970s, a burst that fueled urbanization and environmental destruction, the law prohibits or restricts development in designated areas. During this period Kamakura's population almost doubled—from 85,391 persons in 1950 to 165,552 by 1975 (Kamakura City 1994, 6)—and more than 500 hectares of fields and hills were converted to residential areas. When bulldozers arrived to develop the valley of Oyatsu—next to the symbolic center of the city, Hachimangū—residents organized a grassroots movement and physically stopped the earth movers by forming a human barricade. By attracting more supporters in Kamakura and involving the cities of Kyoto and Nara, the movement expanded and ultimately influenced members of the National Diet from the three former capitals to establish a preservation law.

The preservation law of 1966 contributed dramatically to shaping Kamakura's landscape as "a cultural process" (Hirsch 1995, 23). The measure strictly protects Old Kamakura and its surrounding mountains in three directions, thereby preserving its geographic characteristics as an ancient capital. Furthermore, even in commercial areas, the height of built structures is restricted; tall skyscrapers, I was told, are not compatible with the image of Kamakura as an ancient capital. People complain that the preservation law is inconvenient. A middle-aged female informant told me, "We have to get permission from the city to cut the branch of a tree sticking out from the hill into our backyard." Others say the law embodies the "selfishness" of Kamakura's residents. Mine-*san,* a restaurant owner in his mid-thirties, told me: "It's strange, for these people opposing development came to Kamakura by building houses and destroying nature. They do not allow others to do the same." In my landlady's opinion, the law shows that people in Kamakura are unduly possessive about their own territory: "You know, people in Kamakura are famous for organizing opposition movements." She worries that the preservation law and the ethos of Kamakura's residents hinder development projects that would help the socially weak. Along with other volunteers, she collected a million dollars to build a craft studio for the mentally disabled in a prestigious neighborhood in Kamakura. But the residents are utterly opposed to the project. My landlady said, "Why won't people even listen for a second?"

Meanwhile, Kida-*san,* a member of the Junior Chamber of Kamakura,[8] finds that the preservation law and residents' attitudes are hampering the city's revitalization. In 1985, the Junior Chamber organized a beach festival and held a rock concert there. As soon as they started the concert, however, they began receiving numerous complaint calls from local residents. Kida-*san* told me that whenever a person comes up with a new idea, someone objects that it violates the image of Kamakura as an ancient capital. In his view, the image of Kamakura as an ancient capital also attracts many retired people to Kamakura who do not pay taxes. In fact, Kamakura is one of the most rapidly graying cities in Japan—those sixty-five years and older make up 23 percent of the population (Kamakura City Hall 2004), whereas the national figure is some 19 percent (Naikakufu, or Cabinet Office 2003). Despite the prevalent image of Kamakura as a capital, as Kida-*san* points out, there are very few original artifacts left from the Kamakura period. Almost all of the temples established during that period were either abolished or rebuilt because of fires and earthquakes. Kida-*san* added, "Moreover, they are nothing beautiful—just plain and simple." Yet people keep coming back to the Kamakura period and its founder, Yoritomo. Kida-*san* concludes, "Whenever someone talks about the image of a city with a historic heritage, I say 'There goes the ghost of Yoritomo again.'" The ghost that people keep resurrecting, he adds, threatens the city's prosperity: "Look at the neighboring city—Fujisawa is thriving, with tall buildings, shopping centers, and restaurants."

Kida-*san* thinks that Kamakura should be redefined as a seaside resort: "These days tourists in Kamakura look like mountaineers, with their walking sticks, hiking hats, and waist pouch bags! Tourists used to dress up to visit Kamakura." The city was once a trendsetter—the first in Japan to hold a beauty contest and to have facilities such as a monorail and a highway. Kamakura was a fashionable resort. Kida-*san* strategically uses this image of Kamakura as a resort to downplay its other predominant image, Kamakura as an ancient capital. He idealizes the good old days for merchants—the golden age when they prospered from charging the rich summer vacationers higher "summerhouse prices."

Kamakura as a resort received another endorsement when I went out with Sumi-*san* and her friends. But unlike Kida-*san*, they do not intend to reinvent Kamakura according to its heritage as a resort. Sumi-*san* belongs to a socially distinct category of people in Old Kamakura, descendants of summer vacationers, those who came to Kamakura to rent or own summerhouses. Today these descendants are in their second or third generation, and are often white-collar professionals or employees of prestigious corporations. Sumi-*san,* who comes from the former nobility class, lives in a renovated second home that originally belonged to her natal family. Her husband, who is energetic and outgoing, runs an advertising company. When Sumi-*san* took me out for dinner at a distinguished French-Japanese restaurant with two of her female friends, they recalled the days when Kamakura was a fine resort. One of them, who married a man from a renowned family in Kamakura, told me: "'The true Kamakura' consisted of narrow alleys [approximately five feet wide] and endless hedges that sheltered large compounds. I really miss those days when Kamakura had nice vacation homes. Today the lots are divided into pieces, and many residents have small, ugly houses." For her the "true" Kamakura refers to the town in its resort phase.

Constructing Kamakura in City Festivals

Contending images of Kamakura as an ancient capital and as a resort are also strategically employed in city festivals. The Kamakura Carnival, held between 1934 and 1962 with an interruption during the war years, constructed Kamakura as a seaside resort. It was the novelists of Kamakura, such as Kume Masao, who organized the event. Originally an outsider, Kume moved to Kamakura in 1925, eventually became a town council member in 1932, and also served as head of the carnival committee. Mita-*san,* a photographer in his seventies, proudly told me: "I served as an official photographer of the carnival when I was young. I remember taking many pictures of famous actresses during the parade." Not all the businesspeople are proud to have worked with famous novelists, however. A second-generation café owner resents the fact that they took all the credit for what was accomplished: "People say that the famous novelists of Kamakura organized the carnival, but it was the local businesspeople, including my father, who did all the work."

The celebration consisted of a Miss Carnival contest, music and performances, fireworks, parades, dance parties, and a variety of sports. The Big Parade, the main event of the carnival, consisted of twenty-odd cars carrying the *kami* (a dragon), the Miss Carnival contestants, and others. Considered to be the *kami* of the sea and water, the dragon suited the carnival of a seaside resort town. The parade started at Kamakura Station, the gateway where vacationers enter and leave. Next the procession marched from Hachimangū, the symbolic center of Kamakura as capital, to the seaside. The climax of the parade came at Yuigahama Beach, the center of Kamakura as a resort, where the *kami* was released into the sea.

The annual Seaside Festival in contemporary Kamakura is a descendant of the former Kamakura Carnival. A member of the Junior Chamber that organizes the Seaside Festival told me they created it by modifying the Kamakura Carnival according to present-day taste. He continued: "Businesspeople often consider a festival to be a burden because it costs a lot of money and effort. But we don't have to sacrifice ourselves to hold a festival." Members of the Junior Chamber aim to bring business to the city and eventually revitalize its shrinking economy by holding the Seaside Festival. In this scheme, the old Kamakura Carnival symbolizes the former prosperity of the city as a prestigious resort, and the Junior Chamber deploys it to advance their goal.

The Kamakura Festival, first proposed in 1961, is yet another descendant of the former Kamakura Carnival, although, unlike the Seaside Festival, it draws heavily from the image of Kamakura as a former capital. The festival began as a citywide spring celebration, combining festivals and annual events that had been conducted independently in different districts of the city (Kamakura Shishi Hensan Iinkai 1990a, 608). Some elements of the Kamakura Festival—such as the Miss Kamakura contest, parades, concerts, and sports—had also been part of the former Kamakura Carnival. Early Kamakura Festivals included other cultural performances and entertainment as well: ballet, archery performances, concerts, movies, a theatrical competition, a poetry (haiku) competition, tea ceremonies, and a seminar on cultural treasures. Yet medieval themes and events, such as memorial rites for the founder of the Kamakura shogunate and his brother, stand out in Kamakura Festivals. Furthermore, the 1961 festival included a procession of 162 participants, dressed as medieval warriors, who paraded from Kamakura's city hall to Odawara Castle in the southern part of Kanagawa Prefecture and back to Kamakura again. A medieval procession was recast during the Warriors' Festival in 1997. The local Yoritomo Club, consisting of many businesspeople, organized a big parade of people dressed as medieval warriors. The image of Yoritomo and his warriors continues to stimulate today's festival organizers in Kamakura.

The Kamakura Festival I witnessed began with a memorial rite for Yoritomo, the founder of the Kamakura shogunate, at his grave in Ōkura, where the shogunate used to stand. Because it is sponsored by the city and the Tourist Bureau, people often define the Kamakura Festival as a tourist event—except for the memorial rite for Yoritomo, which is considered authentic. Although it is Buddhist priests who commonly handle memorial rites, Shinto priests from Hachimangū perform the memorial rite. A variety of political and social groups participated in the rite I witnessed. Municipal politicians, the mayor, and members of the city council were present, because the Kamakura Festival is the city's official event. Members of the Yoritomo Club attended because of their personal devotion to Yoritomo. Members of the local tourist bureau attended because the Kamakura Festival is a major tourist event. Ritual participants all offered evergreen branches to the spirit of Yoritomo, and after the rite they all shared sacred rice wine. The head of the Yoritomo Club then gave a short speech: "We, the residents of Kamakura, owe so much to Minamoto no Yoritomo. I wish for the long prosperity of the city." Ritual participants regarded Yoritomo as a founding ancestor of Kamakura City. Similar to the Kamigamo Shrine rituals (Nelson 2000), the memorial rite for Yoritomo accommodated a wide range of groups with various economic, social, and political interests.

Like the former Kamakura Carnival, the Kamakura Festival includes a parade consisting of musical bands, the Miss Kamakura contestants, the mayor, the Girl Scouts, dance groups, portable shrines, and festival bands. Unlike the former Kamakura Carnival parade, however, the route of this parade was reversed, beginning at the first torii gate by Sagami Bay and heading toward Hachimangū in the north. In fact, the parade was no less than a reverential visit to the *kami* at Hachimangū using the traditional pilgrimage pathway: by starting at the "exterior" bay, and ending at the "interior" shrine, it correctly used the plan of Old Kamakura. The Kamakura Festival, therefore, authorizes Hachimangū as the symbolic center because, according to the city plan designed during the Kamakura period, it is "higher" than the seaside. After the Kamakura Festival parade, Hachimangū became a stage for the presentation of Miss Kamakura representatives. Later, on the dancer's stage at Hachimangū, a woman dressed as a medieval female dancer reenacted the sorrow of Shizuka, whose lover Yoshitsune was chased to a distant place by his brother, Yoritomo. Then, as an old man played the lute *(biwa)*, five women dancers in warriors' dress reenacted an episode of Yoritomo. A middle-aged female tourist commented on the dances: "After all, talking about Kamakura is always about Yoritomo."

The Contest over Meaning

Residents rarely cite images from the historical periods when Kamakura consisted of fishing and farming villages. Rather than giving equal weight to all periods of the documented past, Kamakura's history is strategically and selectively invoked to a build a positive image of its residents. In particular, Kamakura's association with people in power—medieval warriors during the Kamakura period and the national elite during the resort era—has been converted into what Pierre Bourdieu (1977, 187) calls "cultural capital." In an ordinary sense, capital provides people with economic means for production, and profit resulting from production can be strategically reinvested to make more profit. Cultural capital vests people with culturally valued resources and competence for making a cultural distinction, which can be (re)used for producing further distinctions. In contemporary Kamakura, people use the city's former associations with power to produce distinguished images of themselves. And citywide festivals offer grand opportunities for the mobilization of such cultural capital.

Kamakura's "place-making discourses" (Ben-Ari 1995), or the ways in which people construct Kamakura as a place, contrast with those of Kodaira or Tokyo. As Ben-Ari points out, people in Kodaira (Robertson 1991) strategically appropriate the nostalgic images of home villages *(furusato),* and Tokyoites (Bestor 1989, 1993) those images of downtown Tokyo (Shitamachi) as centers of rootedness and the communal values alive in old-time Japan. The key images of Kamakura stem, not from home villages or downtown neighborhoods, but from the centers of political authority, consumption, and prosperity. As a former capital, Kamakura used to be the home of the Kamakura shogunate, or warriors' political center. As a former prestigious resort during the early twentieth century, Kamakura embraced the rich and famous. Place-making discourses in Kamakura, therefore, revolve around a once alive but now eroded centrality in mainstream society.

Furthermore, these discourses of place making become combined with *emplaced* order, which produces hierarchical distinctions between upper/lower, front/back, and exterior/interior zones. In a Japanese house, these distinctions result in a higher valuation of areas away from the entrance and the floor (see Chapter 3). Similarly, the city of Kamakura becomes hierarchically ordered with a higher valuation of areas near Hachimangū, the beaches, the main street, and the marginal outskirts of Old Kamakura. According to the definition of Kamakura as an ancient capital, the Hachimangū area—former home of medieval warriors and the Kamakura shogunate—is considered to be more "interior" and "higher" than the southern communities that used to accommodate medieval merchants and artisans. And according to the key images of Kamakura as a prestigious resort, the beach area—former home of upper-class summerhouses and resort hotels—is a "high" place.

These valuations within Kamakura are repeatedly inscribed onto the city itself during rituals. The Kamakura Seaside Festival, for example, focusing on the image of Kamakura as a resort, highlights the beach area, whereas participants in the Warriors' Festival, dressed in reproductions of medieval costumes, parade on the main street—the pilgrimage path leading to Hachimangū. So citywide festivals are opportunities for (re)establishing symbolic centers within Kamakura. As we have seen, residents of Kamakura—both old-timers and newcomers, both municipal authorities and self-employed people—use images of Kamakura strategically to their advantage. A member of the Junior Chamber, hoping to lure upper-class visitors and prosperity back to the city, promotes Kamakura's image as a resort. Tsuzuki-*san*, a seventy-five-year-old photographer, emphasizes Kamakura's heritage as an ancient capital and reclaims the centrality of Kamakura within Japanese society at large. Thus people compete to give meaning to Kamakura by employing culturally specific emplaced order and historically specific place-making discourses.

Theoretically, this contest illustrates that cultural processes mediate social struggles over Kamakura's image and meaning in everyday interactions and during citywide festivals. As others have pointed out, spaces and places are negotiated in unequal relations of power (Moore 1996; Neito and Franzé 1997; Streicker 1997). Places become the site for power struggles and competing significations; ownership and management of sacred places and ancestral homelands, for example, have become highly politicized issues among many indigenous groups (Carmichael et al. 1994; Oakes et al. 1998; Price 1994; Reeves 1994). Yet competing significations of Kamakura are not mapped directly onto an empty space (cf. Harvey 1989; Soja 1989). Rather, Kamakura's residents shape the city and its places by combining two cultural processes: the historically anchored place-making discourses and the emplaced order. The complex interplay among these qualitative characteristics of Kamakura helps to construct people's lived experiences of place during its city festivals.

CHAPTER 5

The Sakae Festival

As we have seen, upper/lower, exterior/interior, and front/back distinctions resonate with Kamakura's past emplaced on a constellation of ritual sites. By using these interacting frames of meaning, people reproduce as well as construct historically anchored place-based identities of Kamakura and its neighborhoods during city festivals. I shall now examine how ritual has been used to build a place-based identity in Sakae, one of the eighteen neighborhoods of Old Kamakura. Unlike many anthropological analyses, this chapter deals with a neighborhood festival that was not as successful as its ritual actors had hoped. The festival of Sakae employed many of the key ritual actions and objects discussed in Chapter 2 that embody important values in contemporary Japan. It also used place-oriented knowledge and strategies similar to those found in the city festivals of Kamakura (Chapters 3 and 4). Yet these actions and strategies failed to bring a sense of solidarity to the residents of Sakae. Although it was shopkeepers and artisans who intended the festival to construct Sakae's place-based identity as a neighborhood of merchants and artisans, the majority of residents in fact consist of white-collar families.

Sakae and Its Shrine

A twenty-minute walk from Kamakura Station brings a visitor to the neighborhood of Sakae. Although most of the area is residential, it distinguishes itself from others as a community of merchants and artisans. Numerous small-scale family businesses are found in the commercial zone where the two main streets intersect. Some shops on Sakae's shopping streets still maintain the look of a townhouse with a narrow front facing the street and a deep structure containing the residential area in the back. Through the glass sliding doors of these shops one can see merchants and artisans, such as tatami makers and screen makers, working inside. Located along the major roads, the stores are visually and architecturally connected to the public passageways to form a unified space. Shopkeepers and small-scale artisans clearly set themselves apart from the giant supermarkets. The tea merchant's wife told me over and over that opening the shop early is a sign of dedication and professionalism —she opens around six in the morning. She is critical of shopkeepers on her street who open at ten, the normal hour for large-scale retailers. Unlike other neighborhoods in Kamakura, Sakae offers almost all the specialty shops and services necessary for daily life: groceries, liquor stores, hardware stores, pharmacies, gas stations, clinics, realtors, electricians, and restaurants. As commonly true elsewhere in Japan, these businesses form the Business Association.

Typical of a Japanese neighborhood, Sakae has a neighborhood shrine where its tutelary *kami* are venerated. In daily life, the shrine is often used as a parklike place. Some people visit it regularly in order to jog; others visit only when there is a special event such as a festival. Just as some famous parks attract people from other regions while small neighborhood ones are used by neighbors, so famous shrines attract people from all over Japan whereas neighborhood shrines usually accommodate local residents. Sakae's community shrine is not nationally famous but is known locally and receives visitors from neighboring communities.

Sakae's community shrine is located near the center of the neighborhood's social and political activities, close to the busiest commercial area and the Sakae Community Hall. The shrine shares a common structure with other Shinto shrines in Japan, partly because the Meiji government encouraged the standardization of their basic layout (Murakami 1970, 174–175). The shrine consists of torii gates that mark the compound, doglike beasts guarding the shrine space *(komainu)*, a purification sink for visitors, a hall where the *kami* rests *(shinden)*, a ceremonial hall where rituals are conducted, a bell for invoking the *kami*, a donation box, an office that offers amulets and ceremonial services, and the surrounding woods. Unlike the custom at a typical neighborhood shrine, however, the priest and his family live in a house adjacent to the shrine.

The shrine's treasure hall displays four portable shrines *(mikoshi)* that are used to carry *kami* during festivals. A small wooden structure in the compound serves as a repository for old amulets and other ceremonial items. Every year, they are ritually burned on 15 January. In the shrine compound are two small subordinate shrines: one offers protection against fire; the other specializes in good business and the protection of households. As well, there are four former community shrines, moved from other parts of Sakae in 1911 following the prewar policy of allocating one shrine per neighborhood. These undersized shrines were merged with the dominant shrines in all parts of Japan when prewar political authorities decided the majority of shrines in Japan were too small and too shabby for the propagation of the national ideology, State Shinto (Fridell 1973, 33, 97).

The tutelary shrine of Sakae follows the general ritual calendar originally developed during the Meiji period. These rituals include the New Year rite, the ritual dance, the ritual burning of the New Year decorations, the spring festival, the summer festival, and the fall festival. Residents of Sakae are most likely to pay a formal visit to the neighborhood shrine on these occasions, particularly during the New Year holidays and the summer festival. Unlike in a Christian church, there is no weekly ritual at the shrine. Although it is relatively quiet when no special festivals are scheduled, some residents quickly greet the *kami* at the gate when passing by.

The Annual Festival

Territoriality is the central theme that runs through the annual festival of neighborhood shrines. During the annual festival in Sakae, colorful lanterns with letters representing "Sakae Festival" decorate the main pathway to the neighborhood shrine. In the early morning of the first day, a representative goes to the beach for purification and brings back seaweed and hangs it below lanterns at the shrine's entrance to indicate the purity of the ritual community. Throughout Old Kamakura, bathing in seawater remains a common method of purification. Yet an older man told me that in the past every ritual participant went to the shore for purification, whereas today they send one person for the whole group. Just as a sense of impurity associated with death has diminished in modern funeral ceremonies to some extent (Suzuki 2000), so the idea of maintaining purity for Shinto festivals in Kamakura is not as strong as it used to be.

Later in the morning of the first day, Shinto priests, a shrine maiden, and representatives of parishioners—mostly older shopkeepers and artisans—participate in a ritual in the ceremonial hall to welcome the neighborhood's tutelary *kami*. The head priest purifies offerings and the participants. Then the *kami* descend and offerings are made. A priest addresses words to the *kami*, and a shrine maiden dedicates a dance to entertain them. Wishing for the peace, health, and prosperity of the neighborhood and its residents, participants offer evergreen branches to the *kami*. This shrine ritual is similar to those conducted everywhere in Japan, for they all tend to follow the guidelines set forth by Jinja Honchō, the central nationwide organization of Shinto shrines. Occasionally the ritual order may be modified to meet local needs or to highlight regional tradition. In Sakae, the dedication of the ritual dance to its *kami*, performed in January, is considered a uniquely regional ritual.

After this welcoming ritual, the head priest transfers the *kami* into four portable shrines and purifies the shrine bearers, all dressed in white.

Figure 9. Festival Band Taking a Break

Participants then form a procession consisting of the festival band (mostly boys and girls; Figure 9), a tall, red-faced nonhuman figure *(tengu)* (older man), the resident priest, portable shrines, their bearers (men of diverse ages), the mobile donation box and purifiers (younger men), and representatives of shrine parishioners (older men; Figure 10). As the procession parades down all the major streets in the neighborhood, many women emerge from their houses to greet the *kami*, make a donation, and receive purification for their family's well-being. The act of purification does not require a special priestly status: male parishioners take turns carrying out their ritual duties. During the procession, parents or grandparents holding newborn babies walk beneath the portable shrine to ensure their infants' healthy growth. Collectively, then, the neighborhood's male participants ensure their community's well-being. At night, the portable shrines are carried once again—this time with energy and enthusiasm for a time of celebration and entertainment. Now the main intersections of Sakae are full of spectators.

Figure 10. A Ritual Procession

Festival lanterns light up the scene as bearers physically connect the portable shrines and sing a song about their neighborhood.

On the second day of the festival, younger self-employed men—members of the youth section of the festival committee—organize a children's show and a lottery. Just as the ritual procession expels misfortune and illness from the neighborhood, so the children's show involves the act of defending the neighborhood from evil influences. A monster Mummy Man—similar to a Frankenstein—arrives from another planet and begins destroying buildings in Sakae's business area. When children failed to repel the monster by throwing paper balls, Ultraman (similar to Superman) appears in the dark sky and flies down to save the neighborhood—a doll comes sliding down a rope—by beating the monster until he apologizes. (Apology is a particularly important element in Japanese social life.) Like Yuzawa's festival, which includes not only formalized rituals for *kami* but also informal festivities for entertainment (Ashkenazi 1993), Sakae's festival also has these two different components. Yet these segments are linked by the central theme of the safety and prosperity of Sakae's residents, lending a sense of coherence to the entire event.

After the children's show, the festival lottery excites everybody in the compound. The sweetmaker—formerly the Mummy Man—now acts as an emcee. Local businesspeople donate prizes—brooms, pots of flowers, bags of snacks, T-shirts, bags of rice. The first special prize, a bag of premium-grade rice, goes to the anthropologist. Every time a number is read out to indicate the winner, people wave their hands, show signs of disappointment, or rush to the stage to receive their prize. At the end of the lottery, lucky winners receive brand-new mountain bikes.

On the last day of the festival, women and children dance in the shrine compound *(bon odori)*. Around nine o'clock at night, a group of men, dressed in casual clothes, carry a portable shrine into the compound and sing the festival song. The resident priest reverently removes the *kami* from the shrines and returns them to the altar in the main shrine building. Helpers clean the portable shrines and place them in the treasure hall. The head of the festival committee gives a short speech thanking everybody for carrying out the annual festival successfully. After the speech, people in the compound, bearers and spectators alike, receive sacred rice wine. The following day is devoted to cleaning, dismantling the stage, and removing posters. Bookkeepers record all the donation amounts and expenses.

Expressions of Place-Based Identity

Like festivals in other Japanese communities (Ashkenazi 1993; Bestor 1989), Sakae's celebration employs a variety of ritual acts to define the neighborhood's boundaries and the status of its residents. Special festival costumes and decorations set Sakae apart from other neighborhoods in Kamakura. Shrine bearers and festival musicians wear colorful jackets, while elders of the neighborhood wear casual kimonos (*yukata*) during the ritual procession. On each festival lantern that decorates the portable shrines at night, the Japanese character representing the name of the neighborhood is drawn.

Promoting the neighborhood's image as a place for artisans, shrine bearers sing a version of "*Tennōuta*," a song originally brought to Kamakura during the Middle Ages—in fact, construction workers are said to have sung this song when the founder of the Kamakura shogunate had Hachimangū built. Different versions are transmitted in neighboring communities; Sakae's version mentions the tutelary shrine's founder and the summer festival. Knowing the Sakae version shows the singer's resident status; the place-based identity is embodied in the act of singing. Women do not sing the song, though some of them have lived in Sakae for more than fifty years and could have learned the song had they wanted to. Yet a carpenter who came to Sakae seven years ago from a neighboring community as an adopted husband was singing enthusiastically. As an in-marrying spouse, he learned the local men's tradition and thus proved himself in the eyes of his peers.

People construct their identities actively. During the annual festival, people in Sakae contest the administrative boundaries and place-names imposed by Kamakura City in 1965. The ritual procession carefully follows the "correct" boundaries of the neighborhood, and people use the "correct" names of subdistricts on the list of donations posted in the shrine compound. The poster includes the subdistrict of Wada, an area that belongs administratively to another neighborhood. In the minds of Sakae's residents, Wada is unquestionably still a part of Sakae. These "correct" subdistricts are the "real," functioning social units used for organizing the annual festival as well as daily neighborhood affairs. Furthermore, local merchants and artisans particularly cherish some of the "correct" subdistrict names, as they date back to the medieval period when Kamakura was a capital and employ characters indicating occupational specializations of merchants and artisans. Thus the festival provides an opportunity for today's self-employed families to display these locally valued place-names. The neighborhood festival becomes a performance, not only to declare what it means to be a resident of Sakae, but also to emphasize the neighborhood's image as a place for the self-employed.

Donors, Organizers, and Laborers: A Social Analysis

If a cultural analysis of the neighborhood festival reveals meaningful symbols and values for ritual actors, my social analysis indicates internal tension within the community. The self-employed are central actors in Sakae's community network; they know their neighbors well and help each other effectively. When a tea merchant fell ill and was taken to the hospital by ambulance, for example, his wife simply told her neighbor, a rice shopkeeper, about it and departed with her husband. Her neighbor went to the tea merchant's shop, removed all the merchandise on the sidewalk, and closed the store. Whether they can trace back their ancestry in Sakae for generations or not, the locally self-employed tend to be active in the neighborhood's social and political life, often serving in the neighborhood association, the welfare bureau, and the festival committee. From their perspective, the annual festival of the tutelary shrine is a neighborhood affair and therefore part of their public responsibility. Thus contributions to Sakae's annual festival are considered obligatory.

In many parts of Japan, "native" residents who can trace back their local ancestry for generations dominate ceremonial activities associated with neighborhood shrines (e.g., Robertson 1991, 130). Yet, interestingly, this is not the case in Sakae. Most of those who can trace their ancestry back through multiple generations in Kamakura do not always report that they value their neighborhood shrines (cf. Morioka and Hanajima 1968, 134).[1] It is the self-employed and the salaried employees—independent of native status—who show different patterns of festival contributions. While the self-employed participate in the festival as

organizers, laborers, and donors, salaried white-collar employees contribute significantly less, indicating their minor presence in the neighborhood network. Salaried employees—mostly newcomers who work
outside the neighborhood from early morning to late evening—have
little to do with the neighborhood's social life and politics. Yet among
these salaried employees, descendants of former summer vacationers
(who came to Kamakura to enjoy resort life) do make token contributions to the festival. Socially these descendants distinguish themselves
from the other salaried employees, the newcomers, because they have
accumulated social capital as long-standing neighbors. If the size of the
contribution reflects a resident's parishioner status, Sakae's case shows
that it is occupation and class that differentiate a sense of belonging to
the neighborhood shrine.

The annual festival mobilizes people through the tightly knit social
network of local shopkeepers and artisans. Among these people, older
men serve as festival committee members to devise general plans, while
men under forty-two serve in the committee's youth section to provide
manual labor, organize the lottery, and produce a children's show.[2]
Local women organize children's portable shrines and dance sessions.
Self-employed men carry portable shrines (a portable shrine is as heavy
as a small car) during the ritual procession and the night festival. Many
locally self-employed families in Sakae send helpers for the task of collecting and posting annual donations. Such families typically give larger
annual donations to the shrine ($30–200) than families of white-collar
employees ($0–30).[3] The descendants of summer vacationers cast them-
selves as good neighbors and donate token amounts ($20–30) to the fes-
tival but do not provide labor. Salaried employees who moved to Kamakura after World War II are least likely to contribute money or labor to
the festival. According to a collector, newer families often tell him they
"have nothing to do with the neighborhood shrine" and refuse to
donate. Families of salaried employees are most likely to participate in
the festival as spectators so that their children can have fun. They sometimes feel obliged to show support and make donations—not because
they recognize their parishioner status but because their children take
part in the festival.

Calculating the proper amount for a donation is a complex process.
Just like trying to figure out how much to spend on a gift in Japan, it

means that one must quantify one's social status and relations with others. Among locally self-employed families, it is their wealth, their sociopolitical stature, and their role in the festival that determine the donation amount. An electrician told me that two families of local fame in his neighborhood always donate exactly the same amount—a declaration that one family is just as powerful as the other. In Sakae, a landlord's family with a long history of prosperity and influence in the neighborhood gave two hundred dollars, whereas the tea merchant's donation of fifty dollars reflected his social importance; although he serves in many neighborhood organizations, his family is not ranked very high in the neighborhood.[4]

Among the locally self-employed, every donation is a matter of public knowledge and the subject of much community discussion and gossip. When I visited a neighboring community during its annual festival, I found a few self-employed people criticizing the head of the Business Association for his stinginess in the shrine compound where the donors' names and contributions are posted. A seventy-five-year-old self-employed man from Sakae told me: "If your donation amount is too small, others say you are stingy. If your donation is too large, they talk about your vanity." Those who do not live up to communal expectations may be punished by ritual violence. In a neighboring community, the portable shrines repeatedly damaged a wealthy but stingy landlord's grocery shop. An electrician told me: "The landlord never fixed holes on the shop's outside wall but just covered them up with metal advertisements. Since new holes developed every year he probably thought it would not be worth fixing them." The blame for ritual violence does not fall onto the bearers, however, because it is deemed to be the act of the *kami* inside the portable shrines. Thus bearers talk about how portable shrines become rough, rather than stating that they become rough in carrying them. The annual festival justifies collective violence as a means to punish bad neighbors.[5]

The roles played by locally self-employed people as major donors and organizers indicate the social and political importance of the neighborhood in their everyday lives. The variation in contributions of labor and money ($30–200) speaks to the hierarchy and differentiation among self-employed residents. The lack of contributions—both in the form of money and labor—from newer white-collar families indicates that Sakae is comparatively unimportant in their social and professional lives. The token donations of descendants of summer vacationers indicate their social interest—good neighborly relations—but not political interest. Their contributions show little variation because they have no intention of competing for prestige in the neighborhood by making larger donations. For this reason, self-employed residents with modest incomes generally make larger donations than wealthy descendants of summer vacationers.

Gender has a significant impact on festival contributions among self-employed and salaried employees. Along with its significant function of providing entertainment, the festival is part of the neighborhood's social and political network, where self-employed men predominate. They carry portable shrines; they serve on festival committees; they take care of miscellaneous tasks such as cleaning, traffic control, and coordinating. Meanwhile, representing their families, self-employed women often serve in complementary roles by greeting the ritual procession in front of their homes to ensure their health and well-being. Some women also tend the family business while men engage in festival activities. White-collar families, however, regard the festival mainly as entertainment. Wives of salaried employees sometimes help to organize portable shrines through children's associations as part of their domestic responsibilities. Their husbands contribute even less to the festival; their primary responsibilities lie in workplaces outside the neighborhood.

A cultural analysis of Sakae's festival activities highlights communal values and residents' place-based identities. Although the festival projects images of Sakae as a place for the self-employed, the festival's ideology generally promotes the welfare of the neighborhood as a whole. The ritual procession demarcates local boundaries and purifies the entire neighborhood for the health and prosperity of its residents regardless of occupation or class. Festival decorations and costumes distinguish Sakae from the other communities in Kamakura. Despite the promotion of communal values and common identity, however, the festival fails to reinforce solidarity among Sakae's residents as a whole. While all of these residents—self-employed people, descendants of summer vacationers, and newer white-collar employees—live in the neighborhood, quite a few have elected to stand apart from the effort to ensure the well-being of Sakae's residents. In fact, unlike in the case of Yuzawa (Ashkenazi 1993, 108), the majority of Sakae's residents choose not to participate in the festival.

As in Miyamoto-chō in Tokyo (Bestor 1989), members of the old middle class in Sakae—shopkeepers and artisans—play a central role in promoting the festival's ideology, projecting the neighborhood of Sakae as a communal place. Yet, unlike their counterparts in Miyamoto-chō, Sakae's self-employed feel that their efforts are seriously undermined by white-collar residents who contribute little to the festival. For ritual actors, this lack of participation is a great source of frustration. Sakae's urbanization has led to a division over ritual matters in the community.

Urbanization, Communal Ties, and the Festival

Until the late 1890s, Sakae had been mainly an agricultural village of some one hundred and fifty households. As Old Kamakura became a modern resort for the nation's new elite in the early twentieth century, however, Sakae expanded. Summer vacationers came to rent or build summerhouses; merchants and artisans began to prosper. During Kamakura's resort era (1890s to 1920s), the intersection of Sakae's two major roads—key routes for transporting goods and people—thrived as a major commercial zone. Besides merchants supplying the basic necessities, Sakae provided services and shops uncommon in other parts of Kamakura: a barbershop, an herbalist, construction businesses, a public bathhouse, inns for peddlers and pilgrims, a major clothier. The barbershop and public bathhouse were especially rare in Kamakura and served as sites for socialization and exchange of information among townspeople. Despite Sakae's initial prosperity in Kamakura's resort era, however, the railways built during the 1890s become a more important means of transport than the roads and shifted the center of business away from Sakae. Intensive urbanization during the 1950s and 1960s further changed Sakae's social and natural landscape. In the era of rapid postwar recovery, job opportunities in urban areas encouraged migration of rural populations to the cities. To accommodate a growing number of the nation's middle class, Kamakura developed swiftly. Soon Sakae's agricultural fields became residential districts. In addition to the houses in front, facing the main streets, many houses were now being built in the interior areas. Most of the current residents live in this interior zone and belong to the mainstream, white-collar culture as professionals and employees of prestigious corporations.

The arrival of newcomers transformed community ties as well as ritual networks in Sakae. Until the 1960s, residents of Old Kamakura commonly participated in territorially and occupationally based religious federations *(kō)*. These federations organized religious activities and banquets for a variety of *kami* and buddhas, such as the Inari, the mountain *kami,* the Ebisu, the earth *kami,* the bodhisattva Kannon, and the bodhisattva Jizō (Ōtō 1977). In the Minami community of Sakae, approximately twenty households were active in two federations—one honoring the *kami* enshrined at the neighborhood shrine, the other venerating the Inari, said to protect businesses. Such federations raised funds to maintain the communally owned shrines and hold festivals. These ritual networks often overlapped with the social networks used for accomplishing other tasks such as organizing funerals and building roofs. Until the 1940s, the dead were buried without cremation (Ōtō 1977, 263), and community networks were considered essential for conducting rituals and burying the dead. Similarly, it was important for people to participate in a territorially based credit association for building new roofs; these associations existed in various parts of Kamakura until the 1920s (Ōtō 1977, 199). Furthermore, accounting ledgers from 1903 indicate that households in Minami participated in another form of credit association *(mujin kō),* from which its members could borrow large sums of money by pooling resources within the territorial unit. (It was difficult to borrow money through regular financial channels without assets.) In short, members of a territorial unit commonly maintained reciprocal exchange relations in both the economic and the ceremonial spheres of life. Territorial networks could mobilize people and resources to accomplish tasks that no single household could have achieved. Yet urbanization transformed such territorial ties, as we shall see shortly.

Accounting ledgers of Minami from the early twentieth century reveal how Sakae's ritual networks accommodated different kinds of newcomers. Unlike summer vacationers, regular newcomers to the federation were expected to make a special contribution of food or money. This initial contribution was recorded as "money for joining the group." The newcomer's name was added to the ledger and would reappear in the following year. Newcomers did not have high status, however, and were prevented from representing the parish. Natives—those born and brought up in the community—monopolized the key ritual positions. Moreover, a wealthy landlord kept the federation's communal funds for a year and paid ten percent interest in the following year, which was used to fund the federation's annual banquet. The allocation of ritual duties and donation amounts, therefore, indicated differences in members' statuses. Despite these differences, all were full members of the common ritual network. In addition to the community's intricate ritual, social, and financial ties, residents also shared strong ideas about purity and pollution: Sakae's *kami* were originally brought to the community to confer protection from epidemics; the annual festival was meant to ward off evil and illness. By parading with the tutelary *kami* on major streets in the community, the ritual procession was intended to purify the neighborhood.

The arrival of summer vacationers in the early twentieth century did not threaten the continuity of these local networks of ritual and social interaction. Summer vacationers were never incorporated as social equals because they stood apart from natives both socially and financially. The accounting ledger of Minami's Inari Federation indicates that several summer vacationers made festival contributions. In 1909, a vacationer made an exceptionally large donation—five to ten times more than the typical amount. But unlike those of other new members of the federation, the vacationer's family name did not reappear in the ledger the next year. It simply recorded: "donation from a summer-house." The contributions of summer vacationers were neither obligatory nor rejected; they were simply received as a sign of their goodwill.

A marked decline of the religious federations in Old Kamakura coincides with the era of rapid urbanization during the 1950s and 1960s. Unlike newcomers in the past who joined the local social and ritual network, these white-collar families did not become full members of the community. Certainly they do not depend on the reciprocal exchange relations that had been indispensable in the past. They can easily purchase services from a funeral home for a burial or from a construction company to put up a roof. Furthermore, people emphasize that festivals no longer provide valuable entertainment. The festival used to be a special occasion with special food and drink—especially white rice and rice wine (Ōtō 1977, 190). People invited entertainers to perform and showed films during festivals when residents did not have easy access to movie theaters. Today, however, rice wine, television, and video players are widely available.

Festival committee members repeatedly told me that they no longer have enough people to carry the portable shrines. Often they attribute the difficulty to the declining birthrate and the pursuit of white-collar careers among their descendants. A collector of annual donations complained that most of the new families in his area ("the interior")—85 percent of the residents according to his estimate—fail to make festival donations. A confectioner in his mid-forties told me, "The festival's rejuvenation depends on how many white-collar workers we can involve." In Miyamoto-chō, the old middle-class families dismiss white-collar families for their lack of participation; they themselves use the festival strategically to celebrate their "traditional" culture in relation to mainstream society (Bestor 1989, 255). In Sakae, however, ritual actors cannot afford to dismiss the families of salaried employees; in their eyes, they have to involve more people in order to liven up the festival. Their concern about the festival's success led to more relaxed allocation of important ritual duties to some extent.[6] Natives born and brought up in Sakae used to monopolize these duties.[7] But as a parish representative in his seventies told me: "These days, nonnatives serve as representatives of parishioners at Sakae's community shrine. I myself am not a native. In the past, this would have been unthinkable."

Sakae is not the only community suffering from a declining number of festival participants. Matsudaira Makoto (1994) reports that the high land prices in the 1980s drove many families away from his research site in central Tokyo. As a result, the neighborhood no longer has enough able-bodied men to carry portable shrines. Thus a decision was made to draw heavily on the labor of outsiders while local people organize and direct them. The festival is continued—and rejuvenated—particularly with the help of many young women who carry portable shrines and enjoy festivals as a kind of sport. Similarly, Scott Schnell notes that in Furukawa of central Japan the movement of families away from the center of town has led to weaker financial support and a loss of younger talents, which threatens the smooth transmission of the festival tradition to future generations (1999, 278–279). Coping with demographic changes in the community, girls are now allowed to play certain ritual roles that were previously limited to boys. In Old Kamakura, though carrying portable shrines used to be strictly a man's job, several communities now use a small number of women. In Sakae, a few nonresident women (relatives and friends of residents) served as bearers of portable shrines during the night festival. In addition, some communities also employ male students as festival helpers.

In Sakae, lack of participation among newcomers embittered ritual actors, particularly because the festival committee had recently expanded the parade route to draw more attention and involve people in the newcomer territories. When the procession passed through the commercial districts, many residents stood at the roadside to greet the *kami* and encourage the participants. Yet as we moved deeper into the residential districts, few people were present. In some sections, in fact, roads were empty. The ritual procession took about four hours of carrying exceptionally heavy portable shrines on a hot summer day. Simply following the procession throughout the afternoon exhausted me— and I was carrying only a video camera, a camera, a note pad, and a pen. After the neighborhood festival, the committee circulated a written commentary among the residents of Sakae asking whether they had seen the procession and participated in the festival. Residents were then urged to take part in the next year's festival.

Ritualization is a strategic way of acting (Bell 1992, 74), but the impact of Sakae's festival was sharply diminished because most residents, in fact, failed to see the event. The festival as an opportunity for bonding and building solidarity differs from situations such as drinking together in a bar. Neighborhood festivals are public events, communally funded and conducted in communal spaces. Yet this communal effort— for and about the community—went unnoticed and hence unappreciated by the majority. The ritual act of defending the neighborhood from evil influences seemed unimportant to most.

If merchants and artisans in Sakae were more prosperous, they might decide simply to ignore the newcomers and celebrate the festival in their own circle. The shopping street in Miyamoto-chō seemed much more prosperous, by contrast, and residents' morale seemed high during the festival (Bestor 1989). In Old Kamakura, too, the festivals were livelier in the healthier shopping districts. In Sakae, however, the economic situation is grim and morale is low. I conducted my fieldwork several years after Japan's "bubble" era characterized by fast-paced and competitive consumption, when the nation became famous for being such an exceptionally expensive place. The insignificant donation amounts in Sakae—ranging between twenty and three hundred dollars—puzzled fellow Japan specialists. Although the Japanese economy began slowing down during the early 1990s, the nation still maintained thriving consumers; it was easy to spend three hundred dollars just for dinner in Tokyo. The image of prosperous consumers and my observations of the festival in Sakae were inconsistent. Sakae's shopping street, once a thriving commercial district of Kamakura, was struggling. Inconveniently located for commuters as well as tourists, and no longer offering services and commodities that are hard to find in Kamakura, Sakae has lost the battle for the yen. Many merchants and artisans in Sakae feel they were left behind in the era of prosperity. A baker described Sakae's shopping street, which lacks stores here and there, as looking like a broken comb. Not only their shopping street but their festival, too, is but a faint reminder of their glorious past. Residents' relatives and children used to rush back to Sakae during the neighborhood festival; guests flooded into town; banquets were celebrated everywhere. Today the self-employed regret that Sakae's festival is no longer very splendid.

Strategies of Recovery

Sakae's festival presents several parallels to Clifford Geertz's description of a funeral in a small town in eastern Central Java (1973, 169). In both of these territorially based rituals, despite their promotion of cultural ideologies, internal stratification among residents gives rise to social tension rather than solidification.[8] Although the division among Sakae's residents derives largely from class and occupation rather than from political differences, "the incongruity between the cultural framework of meaning and the patterning of social interaction" (Geertz 1973, 169) creates social tension during Sakae's neighborhood festival (cf. Ashkenazi 1993, 151). Contrary to its ideology, the festival of Sakae failed to bring about a strong sense of solidarity between the old middle class and the nation's new middle class in the neighborhood (cf. Durkheim 1965 [1915]; Gluckman 1954; Radcliffe-Brown 1939).

Rather than perpetuating static social relations in a static society, rituals respond to social change. Sakae's festival, however, has failed to adapt to the new patterns of social relations that have emerged since the period of rapid urbanization. New white-collar families, for example, have not been fully integrated into the festival. Unlike Kamigamo Shrine in Kyoto (Nelson 2000), Sakae's tutelary shrine is known locally but lacks the national prestige that could be used to attract white-collar families for status-enhancing rituals. Kamigamo Shrine's prestige appeals to a variety of groups "ranging from the descendants of the founding Kamo clan to community women's groups, electric utility companies, elementary schools, local politicians, Kyoto's famous tea ceremony schools, Boy Scout troops, and, most significant economically, the local tourist industry" (Nelson 2000, 11). In Sakae, however, families of white-collar employees and professionals use the nationally famous Hachimangū for children's life-cycle rites to enhance their family status.

The development of commercialized rituals represents another possible solution to the changing community ties. In the case of funeral rites, commercialized ceremonies have replaced the collective rituals that used to "usher the [dangerously polluting] deceased's spirit safely to the other world" (Suzuki 2000, 4). Indeed, with urbanization and the arrival of mass consumerism, the funeral industry has come to monopolize the knowledge of death and specialize in handling corpses. Clearly this industry has taken over ritual services that the community network used to provide. Unlike funerals, however, neighborhood festivals have been only moderately commercialized—for example, by drawing on outsiders' labor.[9] Sakae's limited financial resources make large-scale commercialization of their festival difficult.

Yet self-employed people have not passively accepted the decline of their festival. Lacking fame or financial prosperity, Sakae's self-employed have turned to socialization as a way of coping with the new patterns of social relations: they have intensified the use of children's portable shrines and added a night procession. When I asked why children's processions were held twice, both during the day and also at night, a shopkeeper replied, "The night festival is very special, and we want kids to learn the taste of the festival." To ensure a good supply of ritual participants, the festival committee recruits children from white-collar families as shrine bearers. Thus the lack of participation among white-collar employees in Sakae is not used to contest their membership in the community or their predominance in mainstream society (cf. Bestor 1989). Sakae's self-employed have a long-term plan to revitalize the festival by training future generations of white-collar families through early social-ization. This solution is promising. New white-collar families are more likely to give festival donations for children's entertainment when their own children carry portable shrines or play in the festival band. Yet the most uncertain factor lies in whether these children from white-collar families will remain in the neighborhood when they grow up. By organizing children's festival processions, the locally self-employed show their longing for the return of their prosperous days.

CHAPTER 6

Reconsidering Ritual

So nowadays all culture is power. It used to be that everything maintained the social solidarity. Then for a while everything was economic or adaptatively advantageous. We seem to be on a great spiritual quest for the purposes of cultural things. (Sahlins 1999, vi)

In his critiques of postmodern anthropology, Marshall Sahlins points out the tendency among anthropologists to take "the actual cultural content for the mere appearance of a more profound and generic function" (1999, vi). Rather than dismissing the particularity of cultural forms, this book has paid close attention to the specificity of rituals as cultural forms and how they figure in relation to their effects and purposes. With this emphasis in mind, it is time to synthesize my findings. But I also want to address several major issues in the anthropological study of ritual—such as whether ritual comprises a special domain as opposed to social life in general, whether ritual communicates or not, whether ritual is purely symbolic and thus has no instrumental value, and also questions regarding power.

Rituals in Kamakura involve many layers of embodied and emplaced meaning. One of the layers examined in this book generates meaning from the orderliness found in everyday bodily and place-related practices (Chapters 2 and 3) such as bowing, presenting a gift, and maintaining vertical and horizontal hierarchies within a place. Cultural meaning rooted in these practices can make ritual emotionally engaging by evoking what feels good and right in everyday life. Thus ritual's potential goes beyond a cognitive function that fuses what is and should be "really real" (Geertz 1973, 112). Rituals also involve a variety of bodily and place-related practices that are strictly confined to ritual occasions, thereby distinguishing ritual from nonritual life. Further-more, historically anchored discourses of Kamakura as a former capital and a resort have become sources of meaning for ritual participants (Chapter 4). During rituals, people strategically use places within Kama-kura and links between them to construct images of Kamakura and their communal identity. Thus ritual actors can draw from multiple layers of meaning during a single ritual.

Yet the layers of meanings cited here do not have equal importance to all.[1] Rituals are not texts open to an infinite number of interpreta-tions. Participants have unequal access to the various layers involved in rituals: for example, a newcomer to Kamakura is not likely to be aware of the diverse images of Kamakura and its emplaced meanings. The mean-ings embodied and emplaced in facing *kami* or buddhas depend on the ritual actor's knowledge about Kamakura as well as the religious his-tory, objects, and institutions related to a specific ritual occasion. Polit-ical authorities may endorse one layer of meanings over another to their advantage. This strategic use of ritual offers further insight into what scholars have reported: there is a great diversity in people's interpreta-tion of rituals or ritual sites (see Fernandez 1965; Martinez 1995; Nelson 2000). Multiple layers of meaning and uneven access to them contribute to this diversity.

Ritual's power, then, derives from the following characteristics. First, ritual involves the strategic creation of a context by playing on rela-tionships common in daily life.[2] In Kamakura, for example, rituals draw upon such relationships as the front/back of the body, the upper/lower parts of a place, the beach zone/Hachimangū zone, and former summer vacationers/natives. As Roberto DaMatta observes: "to rethink rites, therefore, we must first de-ritualize" (1977, 264). Thus it is essential to examine ritual contexts in relation to daily life.

Second, ritual has the power of orientation—it orients participants beyond the immediate ritual environment and the immediate actions being undertaken. The relationships that are engaged during rituals—upper/lower, front/back, and interior/exterior distinctions—resemble key frames of reference in Japanese worldview, self/other relations, and social organizations described by Japan specialists (see, e.g., Bachnik and Quinn 1994; Hendry 1993; Kondo 1990; Lebra 1996; Ohnuki-Tierney 1984; Rosenberger 1989). Furthermore, moral values embodied and emplaced during rituals, such as indebtedness to others, interpersonal dependence, and purity, are widely found in other social settings in Japan:[3] in an ethics retreat, workplaces (Kondo 1990), schools (Benjamin 1997), and organizations of the so-called New Religions (see, e.g., McVeigh 1997).[4] Ritual, therefore, links ritual actors to other aspects of social life.

This brings me to the third point: ritual not only links but differentiates (cf. Bell 1992; J. Z. Smith 1987, 109). Often it creates contexts that are set apart from nonritual contexts. In order to produce differentiation, rituals involve bodily and place-related practices that are confined to—and therefore symbolize—ritual occasions.

Fourth, ritual adopts practices that are already formalized and routinized in daily life. By removing their shoes, for example, people create a boundary between the "pure" home inside and the "dirty" world outside. The inside/outside distinction is important in Japanese social organization in general. Similarly, bowing is a formal action that is also part of the daily routine. Therefore, what is already formal and routine in daily life establishes another level of formalization and routinization in the ritual context. In other words, people doubly formalize and routinize on ritual occasions.

And fifth, the creation of ritual contexts involves elevation: they are "higher" than everyday contexts. In Kamakura, a sense of elevation derives from the structures of the body and the ritual environment. Vertical as well as horizontal hierarchies vested in the body and the place represent resources for creating elevation. To produce higher contexts, ritual actors also use the relations among places inside Kamakura— Hachimangū in the north, the bay in the south, and the liminal outskirts of the city. A rice offering made in a "higher" place in Kamakura elevates itself above the mundane rice for this morning's breakfast.

Thus mere repetition, formality, or symbolic elements alone fail to make activities ritual. As Jack Goody (1977, 28) points out: "'Routinisation,' regularization, repetition, lie at the basis of social life itself." He continues: "We hardly need the concept 'ritual' to deal with table manners, or courting behavior, or personal idiosyncrasies; indeed to bring them together under one such heading in no way increases our understanding" (1977, 33). Ritual loses its value as an analytical concept if it refers to any and all forms of repetitive behavior, such as brushing one's teeth, eating rice together, or taking off shoes every day. Taking off shoes is a repetitive act that does carry culturally significant meanings. Brushing the teeth does expresses the values of cleanliness and privacy in American society. Yet these acts lack a sense of elevation. Moreover, daily life is full of practical actions that happen to embody significant cultural values. To make brushing the teeth part of a ritual, it would need to take place in a higher context, thereby commenting on the routine and shining a new light on the act.

How do these characteristics of ritual relate to the nature of ritual communication? Anthropological studies often focus on ritual as a form of communication and action. On the one hand, ritual is seen as a way of sending "messages" (see Douglas 1973, 51; Leach 1976, 45). On the other hand, ritual is seen as a form of action—whether it is considered mere repetitive behavior or an action for social control.[5] Moreover, scholars disagree over whether ritual communicates at all and, if so, how effective it is. Some postulate that, due to their formal qualities, rituals are good at conveying messages (Moore and Myerhoff 1977, 8, 24); others contend they are not very communicative,[6] even camouflaging rather than revealing, due to their high level of formality and repetitiveness (see Goody 1977, 32).[7]

But at this point, it is necessary to ask: who is to *receive* the message? If we regard the subjects of this study as the recipients, ritual is certainly not a signal—like a red light—whose meanings are easily decoded and shared unambiguously (cf. Huxley 1966). Not only are people's explanations of rituals often diverse, but they are reluctant to discuss the meanings of ritual in general (also see Martinez 1998). Thus, as far as messages for nonspecialists are concerned, ritual involves ambiguity that discourages a straightforward relationship between signifier and signified. But what generates all the diversity and ambiguity in ritual's meaning? In everyday linguistic communication, the speaker and the listener can make adjustments and clarify ambiguities in a dialogue. Valerio Valeri, however, points out that rituals do not usually allow for such adjustments because ritual texts—whether oral or written—are fixed (1985, 341–342). As a result, the fixity of a ritual text makes the receiver of the message "understand" what he or she projects onto the text. In other words, the speaker (whether it is a real person or not) does not have a chance to clarify what the ritual is intended to signify. In these ritual contexts, I must add, the community of recipients is not allowed to hammer out the meaning of ritual among themselves. If we were to replace fixed ritual texts with prescribed ritual actions,[8] these points would apply as well to the case of Kamakura.

Nonetheless, the meanings that people project onto ritual forms are patterned. In Kamakura, rituals may communicate many layers of meaning ranging from cultural values embodied in action and place (Chapters 2, 3) to images of communities and their residents (Chapters 4, 5). Rituals can convey significant values in a society, yet their symbolic potential alone does not make the communication of "messages" successful (Chapter 5). Furthermore, as we have seen, access to these layers of meaning is uneven—yet another contribution to diversity in ritual's meaning. Thus, ritual involves patterned diversity and, consequently, a measure of ambiguity.

Limited ambiguity allows room for flexibility, play, and strategic interpretations of ritual. In Kamakura, multiple layers of ritual's meanings may combine to address the meaning and identity of Kamakura as a place (Chapter 4), or the neighborhood's and its residents' identities (Chapter 5). In such contexts, rituals may become vehicles for making statements about what kind of place Kamakura is and who its residents are. Furthermore, competing representations of a place might be put forward during rituals (Chapter 4). Limited ambiguity in a ritual context permits multiple interpretations of ritual and thus presents opportunities for appropriation by the various parties involved (cf. Bloch 1986).

Of course, ritual is not the only way to make a statement; people may resort to written forms, talk politics in a bar, or launch a debate during a town meeting. Yet rituals often consume time, money, and effort as well as negotiation and mobilization of a whole range of social ties. What is being said during them therefore carries more weight and attracts more attention. During rituals I heard many children ask their parents what they were doing. When successful, rituals have the power to catch attention—which creates a more valuable, powerful context for presentation and appropriation. Other collective forms of presentation, such as demonstrations, also attract attention. Yet demonstrations do not necessarily involve a marked elevation in form. Furthermore, they aim to send their messages more directly and clearly. Limited ambiguity, in contrast, can cause different involved parties to see different meanings in the very same ritual. Thus participants only appear to agree to a meaning projected onto fixed ritual forms. Participants in the annual festival of Hachimangū, for example, might seem to be personally committed to the *kami* venerated at the shrine, as if agreeing to Kamakura's centrality as a former capital or as if accepting the emperor's divine authority.

Because the rigidity of ritual form "discourages inquiry" (Moore and Myerhoff 1977, 18),[9] ritual communication differs from a statement made on an ordinary social occasion, which leaves room for various ways to disagree. Although it is certainly possible to disrupt a ritual, the options for disagreement in ritual contexts, other than radical moves, are limited. It is, of course, possible to withdraw from rituals, which sends a clearer message than participation itself,[10] as in the case of white-collar workers in the neighborhood of Sakae. In this sense, rituals become tests: they illuminate whether people conform to the ritual context. Through negation, rituals reveal those who reject or are excluded from them. This makes it a useful tool for the ruling class in its search to find rebels (or for rebels to find their opponents). In a community, rituals can become an instrument for defining insiders and shunning outsiders. Thus it is worthwhile to study those who do not participate in rituals. And because the ritual context demands that participants follow a certain bodily and place-related logic and sequences, ritual has the power to mold participants' bodies. However, due to limited ambiguity, it cannot determine ritual actors' thoughts.

In sum, then, ritual creates a context with limited ambiguity for appropriation that is set apart from daily life. Ritual is an interesting tool because it provides a context to be claimed (or that seems claimed), whether by those in power or by the oppressed. Its ability to produce a privileged form of difference to empower a sense of order in everyday life, and to provide limited ambiguity, both contribute to its vitality. Nevertheless, ritual's symbolic potential alone cannot guarantee its successful appropriation. Rather than automatically repeating established thoughts and ideas, people strategize with ritual.

In closing, let us rethink what some have considered a puzzle in studies of contemporary Japanese ritual. As we saw in the Introduction, national surveys since the late 1990s commonly indicate that the number of people who participate in visits to ancestral graves and New Year visits to shrines and temples (see, e.g., Onodera 1999; *Yomiuri Newspaper*, 28 December 2001) is at least twice as large as the number of believers in religion. Why do people participate in rituals if they say they do not believe in the religious doctrines behind them? The question arises because of an assumption discussed earlier in the Introduction: belief causes ritual action. According to this perspective, people practice rituals because of their faith in religion and, moreover, rituals express or reaffirm their belief in religious doctrine. In terms of this line of thinking, practice without belief makes no sense. Yet in Kamakura believing is culturally defined as a possible consequence of doing, neither as a prerequisite nor as a guaranteed result (see also Reader 1991). In this context, then, it makes sense to find a smaller number of people who claim to "believe" in religion compared to those who have "tried" ritual actions. And ritual is more than a repetitive act. The processes of embodiment and emplacement help ritual actors to construct culturally patterned, socially rooted interpretive possibilities and to create moments of personal significance and engagement even for those who lack religious commitment. Ritual bodies and environments crystallize a sense of good personhood.

Notes

Introduction

1. According to the 2002 Japan Statistical Yearbook published by the Ministry of Public Management, Home Affairs, Post, and Telecommunications (2002, 745), in 1999 the population of Japan was 126,686,000 people of whom 1,757,000 were Christians.

2. Although technically the term *"shūha"* refers to a branch of a particular religious tradition (e.g., the Takada-*ha* of Shin Buddhism), informants did not always distinguish between *"shūha"* and *"shū."* Some of the religiously uncommitted refer to an even wider category when discussing *shū*, such as Zen-*shū* (Zen Buddhism). *"Shū"* can be translated as "sect" in some contexts when describing a Japanese religion (e.g., the Pure Land sect), but it is a loaded term in the history of Christianity.

3. According to the International Social Survey Programme, for example, a 1998 survey on religion indicates that 35 percent of the respondents named a religion/religions in which they believe (Onodera 1999, 53). According to the 1998 and 2001 *Yomiuri Newspaper* surveys, approximately one in five respondents said they believe in religion (Inoue 1999, 24–26, *Yomiuri Newspaper,* 28 December 2001, 15). According to the *Yomiuri Newspaper* surveys, some 44 percent reported they believe *kami* and/or *hotoke* exist in 1994 (Ishii 1997, 174), and the figure was some 40 percent in 2001 (*Yomiuri Newspaper,* 28 December 2001, 15). The NHK surveys (1993, 1998, 2003) indicate that between 31 and 35 percent of the people reported belief in *kami* and between 39 and 44 percent reported belief in *hotoke* (Kōno and Katō 2004, 57).

4. According to the 1998 survey conducted by the International Social Survey Programme, 56 percent of the respondents reported that they often partic-

ipate in New Year visits to shrines and temples, and some 67 percent said they often visit family graves (Onodera 1999, 56). According to the 2001 *Yomiuri Newspaper* survey, 70 percent of the respondents reported that they visit or visited shrines and temples during New Year holidays, and some 76 percent that they visit or visited family graves during the Festival of the Dead in August and on equinoxes (*Yomiuri Newspaper,* 28 December 2001, 15). See Ishii (1997, 59) for more survey results.

5. Respondents temporarily living away from their families were asked to report on whether domestic altars exist in their family homes.

6. Victor Turner (1967, 19), for instance, defines ritual as "formal behavior for occasions not given over to technological routine, having reference to beliefs in mystical beings or powers."

7. My perspective on practice theories draws heavily from Bourdieu (1977), Ortner (1984), and Bell (1992).

8. For historical and philosophical perspectives on Japanese religions, for example, see Kitagawa (1966) and Earhart (2003).

9. Though comparatively limited in its scope of analysis by focusing on contemporary urbanites, this work in some ways complements and resonates with the study by Ian Reader and George Tanabe (1998). They examined practical benefits *(genze riyaku)* as providing both specialists and nonspecialists with the underlying framework that transcends the boundaries of scriptures and practice in Shinto and Buddhist traditions in Japan's religious history.

10. The mind/body dichotomy has been questioned in cultural anthropology (Lock and Scheper-Hughes 1987; Strathern 1996) as well as in studies of religions across cultures (Bell 1992; Csordas 1994a, 1994b; Sullivan 1990).

11. John Traphagan (2000) uses the idea of "bodily habitus."

12. By reconceptualizing the idea of spontaneity, Saba Mahmood (2001) maintains that ritual forms are socially prescribed as well as cultivated for "spontaneous" expression. Her approach is useful because it goes beyond the dichotomy of prescribed and spontaneous expressions.

13. This observation is consistent with a tendency among Japanese people to respond more positively to survey questions that highlight affective aspects of religions than to those focusing on cognitive dimensions. In the 2003 survey conducted by Tōkei Sūri Kenkyūjo (The Institute of Statistical Mathematics 2004, 52), only one-third of the respondents reported that they believe in religion (30 percent), but the majority (70 percent) said religious feelings *(shūkyō-teki na kokoro)* are important.

14. The state did not fabricate these politically significant rites in a vacuum,

but strategically mobilized a range of established practices available among the public. Ancestor worship is one of such key practices marshaled to serve the state (see R. J. Smith 1974, 4, 36). Moreover, the imposition of patriotic meanings upon certain rituals by political bodies had also occurred in earlier eras. The imperial court and shogunates prescribed official meanings for some rites and dictated that they be performed to ensure their prosperity and stability.

15. The 1940 survey (discussed in Ishii 1997, 9) was a special addition to the regular surveys conducted by the Ministry of Education to measure levels of education among twenty-year-old males when drafting new soldiers. Thus the sample used in the survey does not represent the Japanese population in general. Considering that young people in today's Japan are less likely than older persons to report that they are religious, the result of the 1940 survey seems even more striking. According to the *Yomiuri Newspaper* surveys (1979–1994), for example, less than one-fifth of respondents in their twenties say they believe in religion.

16. This is a complex issue. In prewar Japan, the state did not define State Shinto as a religion, and thus, officially, rites honoring the emperor and his divine ancestors were not considered religious activities.

17. D. P. Martinez' (1998) discussion of rituals in the town of Kuzaki inspired me to reconsider survey results regarding ritual activity in historical and ideological contexts.

18. Meishin Chōsa Kyōgikai (Committee for Surveying Superstitions; 1949) conducted three major surveys titled "Surveys on Customs—Superstitions and Folk Beliefs."

19. Comparing multiple national survey results since the late 1970s, we find that the percentage of people reporting that they believe in a religion has been hovering around 30 percent (Ishii 1997, 4). According to the surveys conducted by Jiji Tūshin (Jiji Press) between 1946 and 1950, the figures ranged between 56 percent and 71 percent (cited in Ishii 1997, 4).

20. Examining *Yomiuri Newspaper*'s national survey results since the 1990s, the Japanese scholar Inoue Nobutaka maintains that the Aum Shinrikyō incident contributed to reducing the number of believers in religion (*Yomiuri Newspaper,* 28 December 2001, 15).

21. Similarly, since the late 1970s approximately two-thirds of respondents report that they visit family graves, and slightly less than two-thirds say they visit temples and shrines during New Year holidays. According to the NHK surveys (1973–2003), the proportion of respondents who reported that they visit family graves once or twice a year ranged between 62 percent and 70 percent

(Kōno and Katō 2004, 57; NHK Hōsō Bunka Kenkyūjo 2000, 137–138). According to *Yomiuri Newspaper* surveys (1979–1994, 2001), the proportion of respondents who said they visit shrines or temples during New Year holidays ranged between 56 percent and 70 percent (Ishii 1997, app. 171, *Yomiuri Newspaper*, 28 December 2001, 15).

22. I have no intention of making a generalization regarding the impact of the investigator's ethnicity on informants' explanations of their practice, but this observation opens up an interesting path for further investigation.

23. Due to a lack of staff and access, however, coverage was uneven. In particular, rituals requiring an invitation (such as weddings) are not well represented.

24. The idea of Kamakura as a former capital is a contested issue, since residents of Kyoto, in particular, define capital *(miyako)* as the residential place for the emperor (Umesao 1992).

25. Kamakura attracted a number of nobility, politicians, bankers, military officers, and wealthy merchants of the time.

26. Most of the local businesspeople are small-scale retailers and service providers.

27. *Omanjū* is a popular Japanese sweet with a creamy red-bean center covered with a slightly shiny skin.

Chapter 1: *Kami,* Buddhas, and Ancestors

1. Winston Davis (1992) cites two major frameworks for membership in religious organizations in Japan: obligation and motivation. Members with obligated membership belong to religious organizations because they are required to for one reason or another. Motivated membership, in contrast, is more individualized, and members often cite a purpose for their membership—to cure illness, to solve family problems, to improve financial conditions, and the like. Here I applied Davis' ideas of obligation and motivation to examine people's reasons for ritual participation for analytical purposes. In practice, these modes of participation are not mutually exclusive.

2. This is an unusual practice; the majority of the Japanese people enshrine ancestors at the Buddhist family altar.

3. Ritual practices for vengeful *kami* developed in the imperial court during the Heian period (794–1185).

4. This view should not be confused with a lack of ego, self, or individuality.

5. In my 1996 survey (N = 142; N = 74 in Kamakura), respondents were

asked to identify "important places" *(taisetsuna basho)* enshrining *kami* and *hotoke* that they themselves consider significant.

6. Ancestral graves of parishioners are often located in the compounds of their family temples.

7. Owners of the *kamidana* numbered 53 percent for a neighborhood in Tokyo in 1951 (Dore 1958, 300); 52 percent in Mitaka City, located west of Tokyo, in 1968 (Morioka 1975, 52); 50 percent in Tokyo in 1955 (cited in R. J. Smith 1974, 88); 61 percent for blue-collar residents of Tokyo; 43 percent for white-collar residents of Tokyo; and 95 percent in an agricultural village in Yamanashi Prefecture between 1964 and 1965 (Morioka 1970, 153). Altar possession rates in more recent national surveys were 62 percent in 1981 and 54 percent in 1995 (cited in Ishii 1997, 66).

8. Some 37 percent of all the altars (forty-one cases) receive daily offerings, while 29 percent receive offerings only twice a month (on the first and the fifteenth). Some 22 percent of the altars receive offerings only for the New Year's celebration. As for greetings, 37 percent receive greetings every day, 22 percent twice a month, and 17 percent only at the New Year. Some 12 percent reported that they never greet the *kami* at the domestic altar.

9. Of the males, twelve respondents reported that they greet the *kamidana* every day or twice a month; nine persons said they do so annually or not at all. Of the females, twelve respondents reported that they greet the *kamidana* every day or twice a month; three said they do so annually or not at all. According to the 2×2 chi-square test, $p \leq 0.15149$.

10. Among the forty-one altars I surveyed, women are mentioned thirty-three times whereas men are mentioned only nineteen times for regular offerings. For the New Year offering, women are mentioned twenty-nine times and men twenty-six times. For regular cleaning, women are mentioned thirty-seven times and men only seventeen times. For the end-of-the-year cleaning, women are mentioned twenty-nine times, while men are mentioned twenty times.

11. Married-out and branched-out siblings continue to interact with members of the original stem family as relatives, though cultural distinctions are made between them.

12. While such examples personify places where ancestors reside, place-names are used to refer to people. The head priest of Kōyōji Temple is called Kōyōji-*san,* for example. Personification of places and a place-oriented representation of persons are consistent with the common Japanese cultural practice of merging persons and places (see also Lebra 1996).

13. According to the survey (N = 74) I conducted in Kamakura, most people reported that they rarely or never make petitions at family graves (51 percent), whereas some said they always or almost always make petitions (35 percent).

14. Among the fifty-five family altar owners, the figures for the rest of the altars were 1 or 2 times a week (4 percent); 1 or 2 times a month (4 percent); 5 to 7 times a year (4 percent); 3 or 4 times a year (2 percent); 1 or 2 times a year (13 percent); and never (2 percent).

15. According to my survey, of fifty-five family altar owners, some 64 percent make offerings every day, 7 percent once or twice a week, 5 percent once or twice a month, and 18 percent one to seven times a year.

16. This shop sells modern family altars that look like cabinets. These "new-style" altars blend into modern carpeted rooms with sofas, chairs, and coffee tables.

17. According to the 2 x 2 chi-square test, this hypothesis is supported (p ≤ 0.00097). In my survey (N = 55), twenty-three altars had only one caretaker for daily offerings while thirty-one had multiple caretakers; for regular cleaning, forty altars had only one caretaker and fifteen had multiple caretakers. For offerings at the Festival of the Dead, thirty-four had only one caretaker and twenty had multiple caretakers.

18. Of the male respondents, twenty-three reported that they greet their ancestors every day or weekly; eight do so twice a month or less often. Of the female respondents, eighteen reported that they greet their ancestors every day or weekly; five said that they do so bimonthly or less often. According to the 2 x 2 chi-square test, p ≤ 0.72958.

19. Among fifty-five altars surveyed, women are mentioned fifty-eight times as making regular offerings while men are mentioned twenty-four times. For regular cleaning, women are mentioned fifty-eight times, and men fourteen times. For offerings at the Festival of the Dead, women are mentioned fifty-seven times, and men twenty times.

20. The successor inherits the right (and the responsibility) to maintain the grave and provide ceremonial care for the family dead. Conventionally the successor, but no other married siblings, gains the right to be buried in the family grave.

Chapter 2: Embodying Moral Order

1. Walter Edwards' work (1989) on Japanese weddings explicitly discusses notions of moral character in a form of ideal personhood in Japanese society.

2. Anita Jacobson-Widding (1997) points out that the sense of morality pervasive in the West depends on an individualistic, egalitarian conception of personhood. She examines how morality has a different construction in a place where hierarchical ideas of personhood predominate.

3. According to my survey, respondents (N = 81) reported that they bow to *kami* to greet them (35 percent), to show respect (22 percent), to be polite (17 percent), to thank (6 percent), to petition (6 percent), and to pray (4 percent). Respondents (N = 109) bow to ancestors for similar reasons: to greet them (27 percent), to show respect (19 percent), to thank (11 percent), to petition (10 percent), and to be polite (9 percent).

4. Emiko Ohnuki-Tierney (1987, 143) suggests that cleaning the body and the house are purification rituals in secular contexts. I agree with this view that cleaning involves the moral value of purity, but here I want to distinguish between cleaning and purification. For analytical purposes, I employ the term "cleaning" to refer to order-restoring acts strongly associated with their practical value; the term "purification," by contrast, refers to actions associated with symbolic values. Some acts, such as bathing, fall into both categories.

5. In large tatami-matted banquet rooms, seats are often set up along many rows of long tables stretching between the "head" and the "tail" of the room.

6. Yet a flower arrangement teacher commented that *hotoke* rest on the calyx of water lilies, evoking the image of the otherworld where ancestors rest. Thus, for her, giving flowers to ancestors re-creates the heavenly conditions in which ancestors are thought to find themselves.

7. According to my 1996 survey of 142 respondents, the following actions were performed by the majority at a Shinto shrine: donating money (85 percent), clapping hands (85 percent), bowing (73 percent), putting the hands together (65 percent), closing the eyes (62 percent), and ringing the bell (56 percent). The following actions were performed by the majority at a family temple/grave: cleaning the grave (85 percent), washing the gravestone (83 percent), offering flowers (90 percent), burning incense (90 percent), putting the hands together (92 percent), closing the eyes (73 percent), and bowing (77 percent). A few people said they chant sutras (24 percent).

8. This parallel, however, is incomplete.

9. During funerals and ancestral rites, people are sometimes expected to chant sutras using sutra booklets, but most ordinary people in Kamakura are relatively unskilled in chanting.

10. Michael Ashkenazi (1993, 111) makes a similar point.

11. Since this study focuses mainly on the views of nonreligious specialists,

I did not conduct a general survey with Buddhist priests to pursue this issue further. This priest's perspective may or may not be shared by others. Yet the ability to chant sutras is certainly required of a full-fledged Buddhist priest.

12. Jonathan Smith (1987) points out that ritual "relies for its power on the fact that it is concerned with quite ordinary activities placed within an extraordinary setting" (1987, 109). He emphasizes the discrepancy, rather than the resonance, between ritual acts and everyday acts: "Ritual is a relationship of difference between 'nows'—the now of everyday life and the now of ritual place; the simultaneity, but not the coexistence, of 'here' and 'there'" (1987, 110). Such a characteristic of ritual invites a person to "think of the potentialities of the one 'now' in terms of the other. . . . Ritual precises ambiguities; it neither overcomes nor relaxes them" (ibid.). My study, however, indicates that ritual involves the relationship of both similarities and differences between "nows" that resonate with each other or differentiate themselves from the other.

13. This statement is consistent with the Japanese moral attitude that focuses on the inner state of feelings (Lebra 1986, 60).

14. I have borrowed the idea of ritual as orchestration from Catherine Bell's work (1992, 220), although, when she uses the concept, she does not explicitly emphasize the relationship between everyday and non-everyday actions involved in rituals.

Chapter 3: Emplacing Moral Order

1. Recent anthropological works increasingly highlight the *emplaced* nature of order, although they tend to focus more on the social and legal aspects of order than its moral dimension (Low 2001; Merry 2001; Smart 2001; cf. Thomas 2002).

2. Brenda Farnell (1995) points out that anthropological theories often dismiss bodily actions as mere signs rather than valuing them as forms of complex, symbolic communication.

3. The upper/lower, front/back, and exterior/interior contrasts are cultural concepts and are treated as such. My examination of these concepts does not come from a structuralist interest in the universal, "deeper" structure of the mind.

4. Eric Reinders (1997) offers similar discussions of the notion of hierarchy embodied in the act of bowing in Buddhist monastic contexts.

5. Front *(omote)* could also mean the center of attention in relation to back *(ura).* In this context, "front" can mean public and formal whereas "back" means hidden and casual. The meanings change according to context.

6. Newer houses in Kamakura might not have a formal *zashiki* room with an alcove, but a carpeted living room with a couch and a table to entertain guests.

7. Among Japanese nobility, the exterior *(omote)* and the interior *(oku)* portions of the house corresponded to its public and the private sectors (Lebra 1996, 149). Similarly, merchants' and artisans' houses in Kamakura usually have public areas—shops or workplaces—in the exterior, facing the main street, while the private, residential area is far in the interior, away from the street.

8. Some merchants' families in Old Kamakura do not place the *kamidana* in the formal guest room but in their shop, which is commonly located at the front of the house (Ōtō 1977, 197). *Kami* are enshrined to protect the family's activity of central importance— business.

9. The emplaced nature of order permeates other aspects of Japanese culture too, such as language, self, and social organization. A series of contrasted place-oriented terms and concepts—such as inside versus outside and front versus back—are routinely used to discuss self and other, social groups, and social contexts (Bachnik and Quinn 1994; Kondo 1990; Lebra 1996). The concept of frame (Nakane 1970) also involves an idea of emplacement.

10. Just as mind and body are not separate entities, so person and place are characterized by their interactive connectedness. This kind of ethnotheory concerning mutual constitution among mind, body, and place is also found in other cultures (see De Boeck 1998; Feld and Basso 1996; Lovell 1998).

11. Is the anthropological idea of agency a folk notion of the autonomous individual in disguise? How is agency culturally constructed, and in what ways are bodies and environments involved in the cultural construction of agency? Such questions suggest that we should reconsider the idea of agency.

Chapter 4: Constructing Kamakura in Everyday Life and City Festivals

1. Residents of Kyoto define "capital" as the residential place for the emperor (Umesao 1992). Although I am aware of this perspective, I use the phrase "ancient capital" *(koto)* to convey the strategic use of this term by Kamakura's residents and municipal authorities.

2. Historically, white-collar families settled in the western part of Tokyo while merchants and artisans settled in the eastern part that lies on a plain near the bay (Seidensticker 1983).

3. During the Kamakura period, the community's beach area was a burial ground. In those days, the beach was certainly not a prestigious, "high" area. Thus perceptions of communities change over time.

4. Devaluing margins of a place is also found in traditional South Asian cities, where the untouchables often live at the periphery of the city or the outer margin of the city's boundaries (Levy 1990, 162–163). Just as the bodily element of ritual purity and a mindful element of morality are linked to structure the moral universe (Strathern 1996, 17), so the place elements contribute as well.

5. Natives distinguish between the descendants of summer vacationers and newer white-collar families by the date when they or their ancestors arrived in Kamakura. According to my key informant, "real" summer vacationers maintained their principal residence outside Kamakura and kept a vacation home in Kamakura.

6. A shogun commonly took secondary wives in addition to his first wife.

7. Singing is a common bonding activity in Japanese social life; both young and old frequently sing karaoke or sing along with orchestral music.

8. The Junior Chamber is an organization for businesspeople between the ages of twenty and forty. Those over forty join the Kamakura Chamber of Industry and Commerce.

Chapter 5: The Sakae Festival

1. Of those in the first generation to live in Kamakura, four respondents reported that the neighborhood shrine is important to them, whereas twelve did not. Of those in the second generation in Kamakura, seventeen respondents said the neighborhood shrine is important while twenty-six did not. According to the 2 x 2 chi-square test, the result was the following: $p \leq 0.29990$ (without Yates' correction). Therefore, older residents do not necessarily consider the neighborhood shrine to be important.

2. This arrangement is common in other parts of Japan; see, for example, Ashkenazi (1993, 99).

3. If we combine the donations made to Sakae's tutelary shrine, the subdistrict, and the band, the total donation per self-employed family is two or three times larger than these figures. Moreover, they sometimes donate goods as prizes for the festival lottery.

4. Rank *(kaku)* in Sakae is determined by a combination of the history of the family's wealth and its sociopolitical influence in the community. Wealth alone does not give a family prestige in the neighborhood.

5. Scott Schnell (1999) examines the ways in which ritual violence during the Furukawa festival in a small agricultural and commercial town in central Japan became a political tool for resisting authority in changing economic and political contexts. I encountered a similar but slightly different case during my

fieldwork. A woman from a former summer vacationer's family told me that ritual processions repeatedly damaged the bamboo fence demarcating the residential compound of her house during festivals. The collective violence, therefore, seemed to have addressed the gap between lower-middle-class and working-class natives and upper-middle-class newcomers in Kamakura.

6. Examining the long-term change in social and cultural aspects of the Furukawa festival, Scott Schnell notes that after World War II more democratic relations emerged in the community, and the festival, formerly "ritualized expressions of opposition toward an exploitative elite" (1999, 264), became more egalitarian in nature.

7. The Japanese term for natives, *jitsuki,* literally means "those who (physically) stick to the land," implying that they are local inhabitants.

8. Although Clifford Geertz (1973) implies that there was an undifferentiated ritual community of peasants in Java before the recent rapid urbanization, in Sakae's case there was no such ritual community before the intense urbanization of the 1950s. The native/nonnative distinction constrained residents' access to ritual roles and opportunities. Furthermore, as indicated in studies of shrine guilds (as in Davis 1976), constraints on ritual roles and resources were not uncommon until the middle of the twentieth century (Ashkenazi 1993, 83). It was not until the Meiji period that a shrine support group disregardful of property ownership emerged (Andō 1960). The festival's ideology in Sakae today operates in a new discourse based on residence, whether temporary or permanent, and deemphasizes property ownership and the native/nonnative status.

9. In some areas of Japan, to revitalize their communities people market festivals to tourists, though they also pay a certain price. In Furukawa, with the increasing commercialization of their festival, local people feel frustrated that priority is given to economic matters over cultural ones (Schnell 1999, 284).

Chapter 6: Reconsidering Ritual

1. These layers of meaning are analytic constructions.

2. I am indebted to Valerio Valeri (1985, 343–344) for developing this point; he maintains that rituals create situations.

3. Nevertheless, the body and place practices described in Chapters 2 and 3 do not represent permanent aspects of Japanese culture. The Meiji state encouraged some of the bodily practices discussed in this study in schools and military organizations in order to produce loyal subjects of the new state (Imanishi 1997). Although assessing the historical transformations of these cultural forms in detail would be an intriguing path of inquiry, here I simply note that these order-

ing principles are historically specific cultural forms that to some extent were shaped and propagated by the state in the past.

4. Helen Hardacre (1986, 21) also highlights the importance of reciprocity and gratitude as central themes in the worldview of Japan's New Religions.

5. Frits Staal (1975) holds ritual to be meaningless repetition, whereas Max Gluckman (1954) emphasizes that it is action for social control. See also Bell (1992).

6. Claude Lévi-Strauss (1981, 672) maintains that "[t]he performance of gestures and the manipulation of objects are devices which allow ritual to avoid speech."

7. According to Valerio Valeri, "since it is impossible to pair unambiguously and regularly the occurrence of a ritual sign X with the occurrence of an effect Y (understanding of the concept signified by X), it becomes difficult to view that effect as purely illocutionary" (1985, 343–344). In ritual communication, "communicative and inferential effects combine to produce understanding" (1985, 344).

8. Fixity of ritual actions does not imply their fixity in a historical sense: ritual forms do change. Here "fixity" of ritual actions refers to whether or not participants are allowed a wide range of alternative actions in a ritual context.

9. According to Moore and Myerhoff (1977, 24), ritual thus is a good medium of expression to convey the questionable.

10. Jack Goody (1977) makes a similar observation.

Bibliography

Aggarwal, Ravina. 2001. "At the Margins of Death: Ritual Space and the Politics of Location in an Indo-Himalayan Border Village." *American Ethnologist* 28(4):549–573.

Albro, Robert. 2001. "Reciprocity and Realpolitik: Image, Career, and Factional Genealogies in Provincial Bolivia." *American Ethnologist* 28(1):56–93.

Ama Toshimaro. 1996. *Nihonjin wa naze mushūkyō nanoka* (Why the Japanese say they have no religion). Tokyo: Chikuma Shobō.

Andō Seiichi. 1960. *Kinsei miyaza no shiteki kenkyū* (Historical study of early modern shrine guilds). Tokyo: Yoshikawa.

Ashkenazi, Michael. 1993. *Matsuri: Festivals of a Japanese Town.* Honolulu: University of Hawai'i Press.

Atkinson, Jane Monnig. 1989. *The Art and Politics of Wana Shamanship.* Berkeley: University of California Press.

Bachnik, Jane M., and Charles J. Quinn Jr., eds. 1994. *Situated Meaning: Inside and Outside in Japanese Self, Society, and Language.* Princeton, N.J.: Princeton University Press.

Basso, Keith. 1984. "'Stalking with Stories': Names, Places, and Moral Narratives among the Western Apache." In *Text, Play, and Story: The Construction and Reconstruction of Self and Society,* ed. Edward Bruner, pp. 19–55. Washington, D.C.: American Ethnological Society.

———. 1996. "Wisdom Sits in Places: Notes on a Western Apache Landscape." In *Senses of Place,* ed. Steven Feld and Keith Basso, pp. 53–90. Santa Fe: School of American Research Press.

Befu, Harumi. 1974. "An Ethnography of Dinner Entertainment in Japan." *Arctic Anthropology* 11 (suppl.):196–203.

———. 1986. "Gift-Giving in a Modernizing Japan." In *Japanese Culture and Behavior,* ed. Takie Sugiyama Lebra and William P. Lebra, pp. 158–170. Honolulu: University of Hawai'i Press.

Bell, Catherine. 1992. *Ritual Theory, Ritual Practice.* Oxford: Oxford University Press.

Ben-Ari, Eyal. 1995. "Contested Identities and Models of Action in Japanese Discourses of Place-Making." *Anthropological Quarterly* 68(4):203–218.

———. 1997. *Body Projects in Japanese Childcare: Culture, Organization and Emotions in a Preschool.* Richmond, Surrey: Curzon.

Benjamin, Gail. 1997. *Japanese Lessons.* New York: New York University Press.

Bestor, Theodore C. 1989. *Neighborhood Tokyo.* Stanford, Calif.: Stanford University Press.

———. 1993. "Rediscovering *Shitamachi.*" In *The Cultural Meaning of Urban Space,* ed. Robert Rotenberg and Gary McDonogh, pp. 47–60. Westport, Conn.: Bergin & Garvey.

Bloch, Maurice. 1986. *From Blessing to Violence: History and Ideology in the Circumcision Ritual of the Merina of Madagascar.* Cambridge: Cambridge University Press.

———. 1987. "The Ritual of the Royal Bath in Madagascar." In *Rituals of Royalty: Power and Ceremonial in Traditional Societies,* ed. David Cannadine and Simon Price, pp. 271–297. Cambridge: Cambridge University Press.

Bourdieu, Pierre. 1977. *Outline of a Theory of Practice.* Trans. Richard Nice. Cambridge, Mass.: Harvard University Press.

Brinton, Mary. 1992. "Christmas Cakes and Wedding Cakes: The Social Organization of Japanese Women's Life." In *Japanese Social Organization,* ed. Takie Sugiyama Lebra, pp. 99–107. Honolulu: University of Hawai'i Press.

Brown, L. Keith. 1966. "*Dōzoku* and the Ideology of Descent in Rural Japan." *American Anthropologist* 68:1129–1151.

Carmichael, David, Jane Hubert, and Brian Reeves, eds. 1994. *Sacred Sites, Sacred Places.* London: Routledge.

Casey, Edward. 1996. "How to Get from Space to Place in a Fairly Short Stretch of Time: Phenomenological Prolegomena." In *Senses of Place,* ed. Steven Feld and Keith Basso, pp. 13–52. Santa Fe: School of American Research Press.

Clark, Scott. 1994. *Japan, a View from the Bath.* Honolulu: University of Hawai'i Press.

Cobbi, Jane. 1995. "*Sonaemono:* Ritual Gifts to the Deities." In *Ceremony and*

Ritual in Japan, ed. Jan van Bremen and D. P. Martinez, pp. 201–209. London: Routledge.

Csordas, Thomas J. 1994a. "The Body as Representation and Being in the World." In *Embodiment and Experience,* ed. Thomas Csordas, pp. 1–23. London: Cambridge University Press.

————. 1994b. *The Sacred Self: A Cultural Phenomenology of Charismatic Healing.* Berkeley: University of California Press.

DaMatta, Roberto. 1977. "Constraint and License." In *Secular Ritual,* ed. Sally F. Moore and Barbara G. Myerhoff, pp. 244–264. Amsterdam: Van Gorcum.

Davis, Winston B. 1975. "Ittōen: The Myths and Rituals of Liminality, Parts I–III." *History of Religions* 14(4):282–321.

————. 1976. "Parish Guilds and Political Culture in Village Japan." *Journal of Asian Studies* 36(1):25–36.

————. 1980. *Dōjō: Magic and Exorcism in Modern Japan.* Stanford, Calif.: Stanford University Press.

————. 1992. *Japanese Religion and Society: Paradigms of Structure and Change.* Albany: State University of New York Press.

De Boeck, Filip. 1998. "The Rootedness of Trees: Place as Cultural and Natural Texture in Rural Southwest Congo." In *Locality and Belonging,* ed. Nadia Lovell, pp. 25–52. New York: Routledge.

DeVos, George. [1974] 1986. "The Relation of Guilt toward Parents to Achievement and Arranged Marriage among the Japanese." In *Japanese Culture and Behavior,* ed. Takie Sugiyama Lebra and William P. Lebra, pp. 80–101. Honolulu: University of Hawai'i Press.

Dore, Ronald P. 1958. *City Life in Japan: A Study of a Tokyo Ward.* Berkeley: University of California Press.

Douglas, Mary. 1966. *Purity and Danger: An Analysis of the Concepts of Pollution and Taboo.* London: Routledge.

————. 1973. *Natural Symbols.* New York: Random House.

Durkheim, Émile. [1915] 1965. *The Elementary Forms of the Religious Life.* Trans. J. W. Swain. New York: Free Press.

Earhart, H. Byron. 1989. *Gedatsu-Kai and Religion in Contemporary Japan: Returning to the Center.* Bloomington: Indiana University Press.

————. 2004. *Japanese Religion.* 4th ed. Belmont, Calif.: Wadsworth.

Edel, Mary, and Abraham Edel. 1959. *Anthropology and Ethics.* Springfield, Ill.: Thomas.

Edwards, Walter. 1989. *Modern Japan through Its Weddings: Gender, Person, and Society in Ritual Portrayal.* Stanford, Calif.: Stanford University Press.

Farnell, Brenda. 1995. *Do You See What I Mean?* Austin: University of Texas Press.

Feld, Steven, and Keith Basso. 1996. "Introduction." In *Senses of Place,* ed. Steven Feld and Keith Basso, pp. 3–11. Santa Fe: School of American Research Press.

Fernandez, James. 1965. "Symbolic Consensus in a Fang Reformative Cult." *American Anthropologist* 67:902–929.

Fridell, Wilbur. 1973. *Japanese Shrine Mergers 1906–12.* Tokyo: Sophia University.

Fujii Masao. 1974. "Shūkyō fudō jinkō no kōdō to shisō" (Practice and belief among people without established religious affiliations). In *Gendaijin no shinkō kozō* (The structure of belief among the contemporary people). Tokyo: Hyōronsha.

Geertz, Clifford. 1973. *The Interpretation of Cultures.* New York: Basic Books.

Giddens, Anthony. 1984. *The Constitution of Society: Outline of the Theory of Structuration.* Berkeley: University of California Press.

Gluckman, Max. 1954. *Rituals of Rebellion in South-East Africa.* Manchester, Eng.: Manchester University Press.

Goody, Jack. 1977. "Against Ritual." In *Secular Ritual,* ed. Sally F. Moore and Barbara G. Myerhoff, pp. 23–35. Amsterdam: Van Gorcum.

Grapard, Allan G. 1982. "Flying Mountains and Walkers of Emptiness: Toward a Definition of Sacred Space in Japanese Religions." *History of Religions* 21(3):195–221.

Grimes, Ronald L. 1982. *Beginnings in Ritual Studies.* Washington, D.C.: University Press of America.

Guthrie, Stewart. 1988. *A Japanese New Religion: Risshō Kōsei-Kai in a Mountain Hamlet.* Michigan Monograph Series in Japanese Studies. Ann Arbor: University of Michigan Center for Japanese Studies.

Hamabata, Matthews. 1990. *Crested Kimono: Power and Love in the Japanese Business Family.* Ithaca, N.Y.: Cornell University Press.

Hardacre, Helen. 1986. *Kurozumikyō and the New Religions of Japan.* Princeton, N.J.: Princeton University Press.

———. 1989. *Shinto and State, 1868–1988.* Princeton, N.J.: Princeton University Press.

———. 1997. *Marketing the Menacing Fetus in Japan.* Berkeley: University of California Press.

Harvey, David. 1989. *The Conditions of Postmodernity.* New York: Blackwell.

Hashimoto, Akiko. 1996. *The Gift of Generations.* Cambridge: Cambridge University Press.

Hendry, Joy. 1993. *Wrapping Culture: Politeness, Prestation, and Power in Japan and Other Societies.* Oxford: Clarendon Press.

Hirsch, Eric. 1995. "Introduction." In *The Anthropology of Landscape: Perspectives on Place and Space,* ed. Eric Hirsch and Michael O'Hanlon, pp. 1–30. Oxford: Clarendon Press.

Howell, Signe. 1997. "Introduction." In *The Ethnography of Moralities,* ed. Signe Howell, pp. 1–22. London: Routledge.

Huxley, Sir Julian. 1966. "Introduction." In *A Discussion on Ritualization of Behavior in Animals and Man,* ed. Sir Julian Huxley, *Philosophical Transactions of the Royal Society* (Series B) 251:249–271.

Ichikawa Chikō. 1990. *Bukkyō shitsumonbako* (Questions and answers concerning Buddhism). Tokyo: Suishobō.

Imanishi Hajime. 1997. *Kindai Nihon no sabetsu to sei bunka* (Discrimination and sexual culture in modern Japan). Tokyo: Yūzankaku.

Inoue Nobutaka. 1999. *Wakamono to gendai shūkyō* (Contemporary religions and the youth). Tokyo: Chikuma Shobō.

Ishii Kenji. 1997. *Gendai Nihonjin no shūkyō* (Religion among contemporary Japanese people). Tokyo: Shinyōsha.

———. 2000. *"Shūkyō e no seron chōsa, kekka bunseki"* (Survey on religions). *Shinshūkyō shinbun* (New Religions newspaper). 25 January, vol. 876. http://www.shinshuren.or.jp/press/press879.html.

Jacobson-Widding, Anita. 1997. "'I Lied, I Farted, I Stole . . .': Dignity and Morality in African Discourses on Personhood." In *The Ethnography of Moralities,* ed. Signe Howell, pp. 48–73. London: Routledge.

Jinja Honchō Kyōgaku Kenkyūjo, ed. 1995. *Shinto no shikitari to kokoroe* (Shinto manners and knowledge). Tokyo: Ikeda Shoten.

Kahn, Miriam. 1996. "Your Place and Mine: Sharing Emotional Landscapes in Wamira, Papua New Guinea." In *Senses of Place,* ed. Steven Feld and Keith Basso, pp. 167–196. Santa Fe: School of American Research Press.

———. 2000. "Tahiti Intertwined: Ancestral Land, Tourist Postcard, and Nuclear Test Site." *American Anthropologist* 102(1):7–26.

Kalland, Arne. 1995. "A Japanese Shinto Parade." In *Ceremony and Ritual in Japan,* ed. Jan van Bremen and D. P. Martinez, pp. 161–182. London: Routledge.

Kamakura City. 1994. *Kamakura City Statistics.* Ed. Sōmu Sōrika. Kamakura: Kamakura City.

Kamakura City Hall. 2004. *Tōkei Kamakura* (Kamakura city statistics). Maintained by Sōmuka, Kamakura City. http://www.city.kamakura.kanagawa .jp/toukei/index.htm

Kamakura-Chō Yakuba (Kamakura Town Hall). 1914. *Chōsei chōsa* (Survey of Kamakura *chō*). Kamakura: Town of Kamakura.

Kamakura Dōjin Kai (Kamakura Club), ed. 1995. *Kamakura Dōjin kai hachijyū-nen shi* (History of the Kamakura Club for the past eighty years). Kamakura: Kamakura Shunjūsha.

Kamakura Shishi Hensan Iinkai (Committee for Editing Historical Documents on Kamakura), ed. 1990a. *Kamakura shishi, kindai shiryō hen,* dai 2 (Historical documents on Kamakura during the Modern Period, Part 2). Tokyo: Yoshikawa Kōbunkan.

———. 1990b. *Kamakura shishi, kinsei tsūshi hen* (History of Kamakura during the Early Modern Period). Tokyo: Yoshikawa Kōbunkan.

Kaneko Satoru. 1988. "Gendaijin no shūkyō ishiki" (Religious consciousness among contemporary people). In *Gendaijin no shūkyō* (Religion among contemporary people), ed. Ōmura Eishō and Nishiyama Shigeru, pp. 77–117. Tokyo: Yūhikaku.

Kasulis, Thomas. 1995. "Reality as Embodiment: An Analysis of Kukai's *Soku-shinjōbutsu* and *Hosshin Seppō.*" In *Religious Reflections on the Human Body,* ed. Jane Marie Law, pp. 166–185. Bloomington: Indiana University Press.

Kawano, Satsuki. 2003. Finding Common Ground: Family, Gender, and Burial in Contemporary Japan. In *Demographic Change and the Family in Japan's Aging Society,* ed. John Traphagan and John Knight, pp. 125–144. Albany: State University of New York Press.

Kelly, William W. 1986. "Rationalization and Nostalgia: Cultural Dynamics of New Middle Class Japan." *American Ethnologist* 13:603–618.

———. 1990. "Japanese No-Noh: The Crosstalk of Public Culture in a Rural Festivity." *Public Culture* 2:65–81.

Kendall, Laurel. 1985. *Shamans, Housewives, and Other Restless Spirits: Women in Korean Ritual Life.* Honolulu: University of Hawai'i Press.

Kimura Masafumi. 2003. "The Contemporary Japanese and 'Family Religion' from the Data of JGSS-2000/2001 and Other Social Surveys." In *Jeijīe-suesu de mita Nihonjin no ishiki to kōdō* (The consciousness and action of the Japanese seen through Japanese general social surveys), ed. Tokyo

University, The Institute of Social Science, pp. 145–162. Tokyo: Tokyo University.

Kitagawa, Joseph. 1966. *Religion in Japanese History.* New York: Columbia University Press.

Kondo, Dorinne K. 1990. *Crafting Selves: Power, Gender, and Discourses of Identity in a Japanese Workplace.* Chicago: University of Chicago Press.

Kōno Kei and Katō Motonori. 2004. "Declining Public Confidence in One's Own Society: 30 Years of the Japanese Value Orientation Survey (1)." *Hōsō kenkyū to chōsa* (The NHK monthly report on broadcast research) 54 (2):22–65.

Leach, Edmund. 1976. *Culture and Communication.* Cambridge: Cambridge University Press.

Lebra, Takie Sugiyama. [1974] 1986. "Comparative Justice and Moral Investment among Japanese, Chinese, and Koreans." In *Japanese Culture and Behavior,* ed. Takie Sugiyama Lebra and William P. Lebra, pp. 43–61. Honolulu: University of Hawai'i Press.

———. 1996. "The Spatial Layout of Hierarchy: Residential Style of the Modern Japanese Nobility." In *Setting Boundaries: The Anthropology of Spatial and Social Organization,* ed. Deborah Pellow, pp. 137–160. Westport, Conn.: Bergin & Garvey.

Lévi-Strauss, Claude. 1981. *The Naked Man: Introduction to a Science of Mythology.* Vol. 4. Trans. John Weightman and Doreen Weightman. New York: Harper & Row.

Levy, Robert. 1990. *Mesocosm: Hinduism and the Organization of a Traditional Newar City in Nepal.* Berkeley: University of California Press.

Little Bear, Leroy. 1998. "Aboriginal Relationships to the Land and Resources." In *Sacred Lands: Aboriginal World Views, Claims, and Conflicts,* ed. Jill Oaks, Rick Riewe, Kathi Kinew, and Elaine Maloney. Occasional Publication 43. Edmonton: Canadian Circumpolar Institute Press.

Littleton, Scott C. 2002. *Shinto.* Oxford: Oxford University Press.

Lock, Margaret. 1993. *Encounters with Aging: Mythologies of Menopause in Japan and North America.* Berkeley: University of California Press.

Lock, Margaret, and Nancy Scheper-Hughes. 1987. "The Mindful Body." *Medical Anthropology Quarterly* 1(1):6–41.

Lovell, Nadia. 1998. "Introduction." In *Locality and Belonging,* ed. Nadia Lovell, pp. 1–24. New York: Routledge.

Low, Setha. 1995. "Indigenous Architecture and the Spanish American Plaza in Mesoamerica and the Caribbean." *American Anthropologist* 4:748–762.

———. 2001. "The Edge and the Center: Gated Communities and the Discourse of Urban Fear." *American Anthropologist* 103(1):45–58.

Mahmood, Saba. 2001. "Rehearsed Spontaneity and the Conventionality of Ritual: Disciplines of *Salat*." *American Ethnologist* 28(4):827–853.

Martinez, D. P. 1995. "Women and Ritual." In *Ceremony and Ritual in Japan,* ed. Jan van Bremen and D. P. Martinez, pp. 183–200. London: Routledge.

———. [1986] 1998. "Redefining Kuzaki: Ritual, Belief and *Chō* Boundaries." In *Interpreting Japanese Society,* ed. Joy Hendry, pp. 213–221. London: Routledge.

Matsudaira Makoto. 1994. *Gendai Nippon matsuri kō* (Thoughts on contemporary Japanese festivals). Tokyo: Shōgakkan.

McVeigh, Brian J. 1997. *Spirits, Selves, and Subjectivity in a Japanese New Religion.* Lewiston, N.Y.: Mellen.

Meishin Chōsa Kyōgikai (Committee for Surveying Superstitions), ed. 1949. *Meishin no jittai, Nihon no zokushin* (Report on superstitions: Japanese folk beliefs). Vol. 1. Tokyo: Gihōdō.

Merry, Sally Engle. 2001. "Spatial Governmentality and the New Urban Social Order." *American Anthropologist* 103(1):16–29.

Mines, Daine P. 2002. "Hindu Nationalism, Untouchable Reform, and the Ritual Production of a South Indian Village." *American Ethnologist* 29(1): 58–85.

Ministry of Foreign Affairs, Japan. 1999. Japan Information Network: Japan Access. http://jin.jcic.or.jp/access/religion/shinto.html. Produced by Kodansha International.

Ministry of Public Management, Home Affairs, Post, and Telecommunications, Japan. 2002. *Japan Statistical Yearbook.* Tokyo: Statistics Bureau, Statistical Research and Training Institute.

Miyata Noboru. 1993. *Edo no hayarigami* (Popular *kami* of Edo). Tokyo: Chikuma Shobō.

———. 1999. *Nihonjin to shūkyō* (Religion and the Japanese). Tokyo: Iwanami Shoten.

Moore, Henrietta L. 1996. *Space, Text, and Gender: An Anthropological Study of the Marakwet of Kenya.* New York: Guilford Press.

Moore, Sally F., and Barbara G. Myerhoff. 1977. "Introduction." In *Secular Ritual,* ed. Sally F. Moore and Barbara G. Myerhoff, pp. 3–24. Amsterdam: Van Gorcum.

Morioka Kiyomi. 1970. "Ie to no kanren de no shakaigakuteki bunseki" (Sociological analysis related to the household). In *Nihonjin no shūkyō* (Religion of the Japanese), ed. Ikado Fujio and Yoshida Mitsukuni, pp. 143–159. Kyoto: Tankōsha.

———. 1975. *Gendai shakai no minshū to shūkyō* (The general public and religion in contemporary society). Tokyo: Hyōronsha.

———. 1987. *Kindai no shūraku jinja to kokka tōsei* (Neighborhood shrines and national control in modern times). Tokyo: Yoshikawa Kōbunkan.

Morioka Kiyomi and Hanajima Seizaburō. 1968. "Kinkōka ni yoru jinja Shinkō no henbō" (Transfigurations of worship in jinja-Shinto caused by modernization). *Transactions of the Institute for Japanese Culture and Classics* 22:71–136. Tokyo: Institute for Japanese Culture and Classics, Kokugakuin University.

Murakami Shigeyoshi. 1970. *Kokka Shinto* (State Shinto). Tokyo: Iwanami Shoten.

———. 1982. *Gendai shūkyō to minshushugi* (Contemporary religion and democracy). Tokyo: Sanseidō.

Naikakufu (Cabinet Office). 2003. *Kōrei shakai hakusho* (Whitepaper on aging society). http://www8.cao.go.jp/kourei/whitepaper/w-2003/zenbun/indexz.html. Cabinet Office, Government of Japan.

Nakane, Chie. 1970. *Japanese Society*. London: Weidenfeld & Nicolson.

Namihira, Emiko. 1987. "Pollution in the folk belief system." *Current Anthropology* 28(4) (suppl. Aug.–Oct.):s65–74.

Neito, Gladys, and Adela Franzé. 1997. "The Projection of Social Conflict through Urban Space: The Plaza de la Corona Boreal." *Current Anthropology* 38(3):461–466.

Nelson, John K. 2000. *Enduring Identities: The Guise of Shinto in Contemporary Japan*. Honolulu: University of Hawai'i Press.

NHK Hōsō Bunka Kenkyūjo (Broadcasting Culture Research Institute, Japan Broadcasting Corporation). 2000. *Gendai Nihonjin no ishiki kōzō* (The structure of consciousness among the contemporary Japanese). Tokyo: Nihon Hōsō Shuppan Kyōkai.

Nitscheke, Günter. 1993. *From Shinto to Andō: Studies in Architectural Anthropology in Japan*. London: Ernst & Sohn.

Oakes, Jill, Rick Riewe, Kathi Kinew, and Elaine Maloney, eds. 1998. *Sacred Lands: Aboriginal World Views, Claims, and Conflicts*. Occasional Publication 43. Edmonton: Canadian Circumpolar Institute Press.

Ōhashi Ryōhei. 1912. *Genzai no Kamakura* (Today's Kamakura). Kanagawa: Tsūyūsha.

Ohnuki-Tierney, Emiko. 1984. *Illness and Culture in Contemporary Japan: An Anthropological View.* New York: Cambridge University Press.

———. 1987. *Monkey as Mirror: Symbolic Transformations in Japanese History and Ritual.* Princeton, N.J.: Princeton University Press.

———. 1993. *Rice as Self.* Princeton, N.J.: Princeton University Press.

Ōmura Eishō. 1988. "Gendaijin to shūkyō" (Religion and people today). In *Gendaijin no shūkyō* (Religion among contemporary people), ed. Ōmura Eishō and Nishiyama Shigeru, pp. 1–31. Tokyo: Yūhikaku.

Onodera Noriko. 1999. "Nihonjin no shūkyō ishiki" (Japanese religious awareness). *Hōsō kenkyū to chōsa* (The NHK monthly report on broadcast research) 49(5):52–67.

Ooms, Herman. 1967. "The Religion of the Household: A Case Study of Ancestor Worship in Japan." *Contemporary Religions in Japan* 8:201–333.

Ortner, Sherry. 1984. "Theory in Anthropology since the Sixties." *Comparative Studies in Society and History* 26:126–165.

Ōtō Yuki. 1977. *Kamakura no minzoku* (Folklore of Kamakura). Kamakura: Kamakura Shunjūsha.

Parkin, David. 1992. "Ritual as Spatial Direction and Bodily Division." In *Understanding Rituals,* ed. Daniel de Coppet, pp. 11–25. London: Routledge.

Pellow, Deborah. 1996. "Introduction." In *Setting Boundaries: The Anthropology of Spatial and Social Organization,* ed. Deborah Pellow, pp. 1–8. Westport, Conn.: Bergin & Garvey.

Philippi, Donald L., trans. 1968. *Kojiki.* Tokyo: University of Tokyo Press.

Plath, David W. 1964. "Where the Family of God Is the Family: The Role of the Dead in Japanese Households." *American Anthropologist* 66:300–317.

Price, Nicole. 1994. "Tourism and the Bighorn Medicine Wheel: How Multiple Use Does Not Work for Sacred Land Sites." In *Sacred Sites, Sacred Places,* ed. David Carmichael et al., pp. 259–264. London: Routledge.

Radcliffe-Brown, Alfred Reginald. 1939. *Taboo.* Cambridge: Cambridge University Press.

Reader, Ian. 1991. *Religion in Contemporary Japan.* Honolulu: University of Hawai'i Press.

———. 1995. "Cleaning Floors and Sweeping the Mind: Cleaning as a Ritual Process." In *Ceremony and Ritual in Japan,* ed. Jan van Bremen and D. P. Martinez, pp. 227–245. London: Routledge.

Reader, Ian, and George J. Tanabe Jr. 1998. *Practically Religious: Worldly Benefits and the Common Religion of Japan.* Honolulu: University of Hawai'i Press.

Reeves, Brian. 1994. "*Ninaistákis*—the *Nitsitapii*'s Sacred Mountain: Traditional Native Religious Activities and Land Use/Tourism Conflicts." In *Sacred Sites, Sacred Places*, ed. David Carmichael et al., pp. 265–295. London: Routledge.

Reinders, Eric. 1997. "Ritual Topography: Embodiment and Vertical Space in Buddhist Monastic Practice." *History of Religions* 36:244–264.

Robertson, Jennifer. 1991. *Native and Newcomer: Making and Remaking of a Japanese City*. Berkeley: University of California Press.

Rodman, Margaret. 1992. "Empowering Place: Multilocality and Multivocality." *American Anthropologist* 94(3):640–656.

Rosenberger, Nancy R. 1989. "Dialectic Balance in the Polar Model of Self: The Japan Case." *Ethos* 17:88–113.

Rotenberg, Robert. 1993. "Introduction." In *The Cultural Meaning of Urban Space*, ed. Robert Rotenberg and Gary McDonogh, pp. xi–xix. Westport, Conn.: Bergin & Garvey.

Sahlins, Marshall. 1999. "What Is Anthropological Enlightenment?" *Annual Review of Anthropology* 28:i–xxiii.

Sawa Jurō. 1976. *Kamakura koezu kikō* (Old maps and drawings of Kamakura). Tokyo: Tokyo Bijutsu.

Schnell, Scott. 1999. *The Rousing Drum: Ritual Practice in a Japanese Community*. Honolulu: University of Hawai'i Press.

Seidensticker, Edward. 1983. *Low City, High City: Tokyo from Edo to the Earthquake*. New York: Knopf.

Sered, Susan. 1999. *Women of the Sacred Groves: Divine Priestesses of Okinawa*. New York: Oxford University Press.

Shimada Hiromi. 1991. *Ima shūkyō ni nani ga okotte irunoka* (What is happening to religion today). Tokyo: Kōdansha.

Shimamoto Kazuya. 1993. *Kamakura bessō monogatari* (Stories of second houses in Kamakura). Kanagawa: Nakajima Insatsujo.

Shimazono Susumu. 2004. "Kindai Nihon ni okeru 'shūkyō' gainen no jyuyō" (The Accommodation of the Concept of Religion in Modern Japan). In *Shūkyō saikō* (Reconsidering religion). Tokyo: Perikansha.

Shweder, Richard (with Edmund J. Bourne). 1991. "Does the Concept of the Person Vary Cross-Culturally?" In Richard Shweder, *Thinking through Cultures: Expeditions in Cultural Psychology*, pp. 113–155. Cambridge, Mass.: Harvard University Press.

Smart, Alan. 2001. "Unruly Places: Urban Governance and the Persistence of

Illegality in Hong Kong's Urban Squatter Areas." *American Anthropologist* 103(1):30–44.

Smith, Jonathan Z. 1987. *To Take Place: Toward Theory in Ritual.* Chicago: University of Chicago Press.

Smith, Robert J. 1974. *Ancestor Worship in Contemporary Japan.* Stanford, Calif.: Stanford University Press.

Smyers, Karen A. 1999. *The Fox and the Jewel: Shared and Private Meanings in Contemporary Japanese Inari Worship.* Honolulu: University of Hawai'i Press.

Soja, Edward. 1989. *Postmodern Geographies: The Reassertion of Space in Critical Social Theory.* London: Verso.

Staal, Frits. 1975. *The Meaninglessness of Ritual.* Numen 26(1):2–22.

Strathern, Andrew J. 1996. *Body Thoughts.* Ann Arbor: University of Michigan Press.

Streicker, Joel. 1997. "Spatial Reconfigurations, Imagined Geographies, and Social Conflicts in Cartagena, Colombia." *Cultural Anthropology* 12(1): 109–128.

Sullivan, Lawrence E. 1990. "Body Works: Knowledge of the Body in the Study of Religion." *History of Religions* 30(1):86–99.

Suzuki, Hikaru. 2000. *The Price of Death.* Stanford, Calif.: Stanford University Press.

Tamamuro Fumio. 1971. *Edo bakufu no shūkyō tōsei* (The Tokugawa shogunate's legal control over religions). Tokyo: Hyōronsha.

Tambiah, Stanley. 1968. "The Magical Power of Words." *Man* n.s. 3(2):175–208.

———. 1985. *Culture, Thought, and Social Action.* Cambridge, Mass.: Harvard University Press.

Tanizaki Junichirō. 1985. *Naomi.* Trans. Anthony H. Chambers. New York: Knopf.

Thomas, Philip. 2002. "The River, the Road, and the Rural-Urban Divide: A Postcolonial Moral Geography from Southeast Madagascar." *American Ethnologist* 29(2):366–391.

Tōkei Sūri Kenkyūjo (The Institute of Statistical Mathematics). 2004. A Study of the Japanese National Character: The Eleventh Nationwide Survey. Tokyo: Institute of Statistical Mathematics.

Traphagan, John. 2000. *Taming Oblivion: Aging Bodies and the Fear of Senility in Japan.* Albany: State University of New York Press.

Tsushima Michihito. 1992. "Shinshūkyō no rekishi to genzai" (History of the New Religions and their present). In *Nihon shūkyō sōran* (Complete guide to religions in Japan), ed. Yamaori Tetsuo, pp. 288–289. Tokyo: Shin Jin-butsu Ōraisha.

Turner, Victor. 1966. *The Ritual Process: Structure and Anti-Structure*. Ithaca, N.Y.: Cornell University Press.

———. 1967. *The Forest of Symbols: Aspects of Ndembu Ritual*. Ithaca, N.Y.: Cornell University Press.

Ueda Atsushi. 1974. *Nihonjin to sumai* (The Japanese and their living quarters). Tokyo: Iwanami Shoten.

Umesao Tadao. 1992. *Kyoto bunkaron* (Cultural analysis of Kyoto). *Works of Umesao Tadao*, vol. 17. Tokyo: Chūō Kōronsha.

Umesao Tadao, Kindaichi Haruhiko, Sakakura Atsuyoshi, and Hinohara Shige-aki, eds. 1995. *Nihongo daijiten* (Dictionary of Japanese). 2nd ed. Tokyo: Kōdansha.

Valeri, Valerio. 1985. *Kingship and Sacrifice*. Chicago: University of Chicago Press.

Van Bremen, Jan. 1995. "Introduction: The Myth of the Secularization of Indus-trialized Societies." In *Ceremony and Ritual in Japan*, ed. Jan van Bremen and D. P. Martinez, pp. 1–22. London: Routledge.

Weiner, James. 1991. *The Empty Place: Poetry, Space, and Being among the Foi of Papua New Guinea*. Bloomington: Indiana University Press.

Yamaori Tetsuo. 1996. *Kindai Nihonjin no shūkyō ishiki* (Religious conscious-ness among the modern Japanese). Tokyo: Iwanami Shoten.

Yanagawa Keiichi. 1991. *Gendai Nihonjin no shūkyō* (Religion among the con-temporary Japanese). Kyoto: Hōzōkan.

Yomiuri Newspaper. 1996a. "Hatsumōde no hitode" (New Year visitors to shrines and temples). 4 January, evening ed.

———. 1996b. "Wakaian o judaku shi 'mōshiwake arimasen' to dogeza shite shazai suru Midori Jūji no shachō" (Having accepted a reconciliation, the president of the Green Cross Company, apologizing in the *dogeza*-style). 15 March.

———. 2001. "Shūkyōkan honsha zenkoku yoron chōsa" (National survey on religion). 28 December.

Index

Note: Page numbers in *italic* indicate illustrations.